The Cultural World of the Apostles

The Cultural World of the Apostles

The Second Reading, Sunday by Sunday
Year B

John J. Pilch

THE LITURGICAL PRESS
Collegeville, Minnesota

www.litpress.org

Year A: 0-8146-2726-9
Year B: 0-8146-2781-1

1   2   3   4   5   6   7   8   9

Library of Congress Cataloging-in-Publication Data

Pilch, John J.
    The cultural world of the apostles: the second reading, Sunday by Sunday, year A / John J. Pilch.
        p. cm.
    Includes bibliographical references.
    ISBN 0-8146-2726-9 (alk. paper)
    1. Bible. N.T. Epistles—Liturgical use. 2. Bible. N.T. Revelation—Liturgical use. 3. Bible. N.T. Epistles—History of contemporary events. 4. Bible. N.T. Revelation—History of contemporary events. 5. Middle East—Civilization—To 622. I. Title.

BS2635.55 .P55 2001
227'.067—dc21

00-052042

For The Context Group

Colleagues, Friends, and Cultural Informants

Contents

Introduction

During a recent extended visit—my third—to Poland, I realized that I was suffering culture shock. The discovery surprised me. I was born in America of first-generation American parents, but my first language was Polish. I am fluent in that language. My formal education included fourteen years of the study of the Polish language, history, culture, and literature. In Poland, people often ask, "When did you return to Poland?" or "How long have you lived in America." They are surprised to learn that I was born in America.

As I reflected upon and analyzed my shocking experiences, it became clear to me that the pain was caused because I was misunderstanding and misinterpreting my experiences. I was insufficiently aware of the melody of the spoken language that gives nuance to spoken words. I also failed to notice nonverbal cues. Gradually I realized that this is a high-context culture; that is, people assume and take many things for granted because every one is socialized to know what is expected in each interpersonal interaction. In contrast, my own low-context American culture has socialized me to expect everything to be spelled out in great detail. In brief, I realized that I do not know the Polish social system very well, for it is the social system that gives meaning to language and human experience. The Polish-American social system in which I was socialized is somewhat helpful but mostly inadequate for Poland.

This visit differed from the others in that I was the guest of a native Pole, Dr. Jadwiga M. Rakowska. She served as a guide and informant. She explained and interpreted my puzzling experiences even though she didn't witness many of them. She recommended a newly published dictionary written for foreigners. I consulted it often during our postdinner discussions to clarify for myself nuances in this highly inflected language. Moreover, the dictionary pointed out that much of my vocabulary is "literary." In modern Poland, a new and different vocabulary has developed. I came to appreciate the value of a native cultural informant or guide.

People whose cultural background is not Mediterranean or Middle- Eastern should expect the same kind of shocking experiences when they read the Bible. If reading the Bible is not a jarring experience, that could be a clue that the reader is imposing her or his culture upon the people on the pages of their English translations. Such a reading tends to make those people "just like us." Any contemporary experience with people from others cultures should make one quite aware of the fact that "they" are not "just like us."

In my three-volume series *The Cultural World of Jesus: Sunday by Sunday* (Collegeville: The Liturgical Press, 1995–97), I tried to serve my readers as a cultural informant or guide. No, I am not a native of the Mediterranean world, but my colleagues in The Context Group and I have spent a good portion of our careers studying the writings of "ancient informants." We have helped one another discover how to imagine the appropriate cultural scenario needed in order to understand and properly interpret the people and their behaviors described in the Bible.

Even as I began that project on the Gospels, I also intended to write a similar series of cultural reflections on the second or middle readings of the three-year lectionary cycle for Sundays. The middle reading was intended by the architects of the lectionary to be independent of the other two readings. The aim was to offer a semicontinuous reading from the letters attributed to Paul (and James in Cycle B, Twenty-Second to Twenty-Sixth Sundays in Ordinary Time). First Corinthians was spread over three years, Hebrews was spread over two years (Cycles B and C), while the other letters were completed within a given year. The letters of Peter and John and selections from Revelation were assigned to the Easter and Christmas seasons (see Sloyan). Though the author of Revelation is not the apostle John but rather one who described himself as a prophet writing for fellow Jesus-prophets (Rev 1:3), and Paul the apostle also casts himself in the role of a prophet (Gal 1:15; compare Jer 1:4), the title of this present book is *The Cultural World of the Apostles*. It treats the second or middle readings for all the Sundays and some of the feasts in the Liturgical Year B.

The notion of a semicontinuous reading makes good sense. Scholars agree that in order to appreciate what a sacred author wanted to communicate, it is advisable to read that author's book or letter from beginning to end at one sitting. Given the time constraints of the liturgy, and the limited number of Sundays in a year, only parts of a letter or document are read, not the entire document. However, the architects of the lectionary did not explain why they arranged these "edited" documents in the order we find in the lectionary over the three years, or even in any given year. That order is certainly not chronological. Therefore, to help the reader understand a given document within the life-setting of its author, I give a brief indication of the probable date of that letter and some indication of the circumstances in which it was written or to which it was directed.

The principle that guided the architects of the lectionary in selecting these middle readings in the Sunday Lectionary was that they be "short and readily grasped by the people." The readings are indeed short, deliberately edited for that purpose. In many instances, however, that brevity has deprived the reader or listener of sufficient context to interpret the text-segment in a responsible way. The reading is invariably torn from its integral literary form in the letter, and sometimes verses are omitted in order to combine what remains into a reading "readily grasped by the people." As many commentators have noted, this process has unwittingly created a new scripture. These high-context documents are now raised to an even higher context! I try to present, as briefly as possible, this broader literary context for each reading as needed. (See, for example, Second Sunday of Advent.)

That the architects actually believed a brief reading could be "readily grasped by the people" is astonishing. Everyone can understand the brief English sentence: "He hit it." But without the proper context, it is entirely impossible to *interpret* this sentence. Who is he? What is it? What is the meaning of "hit"? Many of the brief readings in the lectionary contain but two verses! Try to interpret 1 John 3:1-2, the reading for the Fourth Sunday of Easter, Year B. Then read the reflection in this book. Does your interpretation correlate with the reflection in this book? What was missing? What didn't you know about this sacred author and his community that would make a difference in your interpretation? What kind of consequences would that have for the application of these verses that you would like to make in your life, or the life of the Church?

The architects also appear to have been totally unaware of the radically different cultural settings in which the majority of contemporary readers or listeners receive these text-segments which originated in first-century Mediterranean cultural settings. That culture is the essential context for interpreting what the sacred author intended and meant. Only when the reader or listener has grasped that meaning can the reader or listener begin to make an application to his or her own cultural context. Thus, consider the selection from Galatians 4:4-7 assigned for January 1: the Solemnity of the Blessed Virgin Mary, the Mother of God. Without an understanding of how young boys are raised in the Ancient Middle Eastern world, the interpretation of this passage can easily be overshadowed by Western understanding of the word "Father," and its emotional overtones. To understand the very different emotional overtones a Middle Eastern boy would assign to this word, read the comment on Hebrews 5:7-9 (Fifth Sunday of Lent). Once this understanding is grasped, a reader can begin to explore the cultural significance of Paul's statement and recognize the challenge of applying it in a different cultural context.

Just as in my volumes on *The Cultural World of Jesus,* so too here do I use the historical critical method supplemented by insights from cultural anthropology. One understanding of history is that things were not always the way they are now. Even in antiquity, if a reader can place Paul and his letters in chronological context, it becomes easier to notice where Paul's thinking has developed or where Paul has changed his mind. Moreover, of the letters attributed to Paul in the New Testament, scholars agree that seven are indisputably authentic: 1 Thessalonians, Galatians, 1–2 Corinthians, Philemon, Romans, and Philippians. Because the authenticity of the others is disputed, they are called the Deutero-Paulines: 2 Thessalonians, Colossians, Ephesians, 1–2 Timothy, and Titus. Hebrews is not really a letter (actually, neither is Ephesians), and scholars agree that it was not written by Paul. I indicate this kind of historical information in this book at the first verses drawn from a given document of the New Testament in the lectionary. The reader is thus encouraged to consider how far removed this text-segment may be from the time of Jesus' death, from the time of the activity of his disciples, and even from the time of the reputed author. What has developed during thirty or more years? In the case of letters written by Paul's disciples in his name (e.g., 1–2 Tim, Titus), what developments have emerged?

With due respect to the architects of the lectionary, Paul cannot be "readily grasped by the people" if those people do not share his Mediterranean cultural heritage (see Malina and Neyrey). True to his own cultural heritage, Paul is a non-introspective person who thinks as he speaks. His letters record what flowed from his mouth after a fashion we might identify as stream of consciousness. Mediterranean persons often speak while they think. They do not routinely think before speaking. Hence Paul's letters often seem illogical, contradictory, and very difficult to understand. Practically all commentators admit this.

To complicate matters, in his letters (and those of other apostles) we have only half the conversation. We do not know the statements or ideas or behaviors to which he is reacting. We have only his (accurate? or biased?) report and his interpretation of what others have said or done. The experience is similar to hearing only one side of a telephone conversation. Relying upon expert Pauline scholars such as Jerome Murphy-O'Connor or Joseph Fitzmyer, I have tried to indicate where Paul or another apostle may have been quoting an opponent. This is not always evident in the text of the lectionary or the Bible.

The Mediterranean cultural information I seek to share in these reflections is not generally available in the vast majority of commentaries or homiletic aids currently on the market. The resources and scholars upon whom I have relied are listed at the end of this volume. The information provided in traditional commentaries and homiletic aids is good and presupposed by my reflections. At the same time, cultural insights may require that a reader modify that information in reaching a final interpretation of each text-segment that will respect its original cultural setting.

At the conclusion of the reflections in *The Cultural World of Jesus,* I attempted to craft a question or thought about possible relevance or challenge to the contemporary believer in his or her culture. In this volume, I have attempted the same and something more. Though the second reading was never intended by the architects of the lectionary to be related to the gospel, nearly all the preaching I have heard in all denominations that use this or a similar lectionary attempts to relate all three readings to each other (for better or for worse!). Moreover, participants in RCIA (Rite of Christian Initiation of Adults) programs who have found my previous three volumes very helpful will probably want to relate their thoughts on the second reading with the gospel. For this reason, I have attempted to suggest such a relationship where it seems possible. Readers who use this book in line with the intention of the architects of the lectionary who never intended these readings to be related to the gospel can simply ignore the final sentence or paragraph in which I do that.

My prayer is that this volume, like its predecessors and companion *(The Cultural World of Jesus; The Cultural Dictionary of the Bible),* might contribute to an ever deeper understanding of and appreciation for our Mediterranean ancestors in the faith.

Feast of St. John the Baptist   John J. Pilch
June 24, 2002   Georgetown University

First Sunday of Advent
1 Corinthians 1:3-9

This letter was probably written about the year 54 A.D. from Ephesus. These verses are a statement of "thanksgiving," a customary segment in most of Paul's letters. Of special interest here is that he engages in subtle criticism, paying a left-handed compliment as it were. Ordinarily, Paul acknowledges that God's grace in a community is manifest in faith (Rom 1:8), or faith, hope, and charity (1 Thess 1:3), but in Corinth Paul points to "all discourse and all knowledge" (v. 5). The Corinthians boasted of their spiritual gifts, and Paul does indeed acknowledge these in v. 7. The fact that he does not mention faith, hope, or charity would likely be noticed by the letter's recipients. They were somewhat deficient in these matters.

Notice how Paul emphasizes the initiative and activity of God in these verses. "Were enriched" and "was confirmed" are theological passives. The passive voice is a way of speaking about God without mentioning the divine name. The Corinthians must not forget that their graces are gifts from God and not the result of personal effort and achievement. Moreover, Paul reminds them that fulfillment, perfection, completion are yet to come ("as you wait" for the parousia, that is, the Second Coming of Christ).

With God's assistance, the Corinthians will be found irreproachable, holy, pure on the day of the Lord Jesus Christ. Earlier in his letters (e.g., 1 Thess 5:1-6), Paul referred simply

1

to the Day of the Lord, that is, God. Now he uses the word Lord as a reference to Jesus. But the Corinthians, for all their weaknesses and shortcomings, must remember that God is unswervingly loyal (faithful). God will not let them down after having called them to common union or fellowship with Jesus.

The sentiments of these verses explain why believers ought not fear Jesus' exhortation to vigilance in today's gospel (Mark 13:33-37). God is loyal to those who serve the deity faithfully. Such have nothing to fear or worry about.

Second Sunday of Advent
2 Peter 3:8-14

This pseudonymous letter is more in the form of a farewell address than an epistle (for other farewell addresses in the New Testament see Mark 13 and parallels; John 13–17; Acts 20:17-35; 2 Timothy). It therefore presumes to be Peter's "last will and testament," as it were, and in content it most closely resembles Jude. It is most likely the latest composition of the New Testament written sometime in the first quarter of the second century by someone in Peter's name.

False teachers have denied the Lord's power and authority and scoffed at the Lord's coming. In these verses, the pseudonymous author presents reasons for the delayed return of the Lord (vv. 8-9) and the implications this has on Christian behavior (vv. 10-13). Time, as we know, is a mental fiction with a foundation in reality. If time were real, we could not "spring" forward or "fall" back, nor could we call "time out." Nevertheless, the mental fiction controls life in every culture. As anthropologists observe, that which functions as reality is real. Thus, the sacred author argues against the scoffers by noting that God who lives outside time measures it differently than humans (with the Lord one day is like a thousand years, see Ps 90:4). Further, what appears to be "delay" is a sign of patience. He allows plenty of opportunity for repentance.

The next verses (10-13) concern behavior rather than details of the end. Nowhere else does the Bible mention a final

3

conflagration of all that exists, but this notion does reflect Greek thought. Association of fire with the day of the Lord and final judgment (e.g., Isa 66:15-18; Mal 4:1; Zeph 1:18) probably contributed to the blending of Israelite and Greek imagery (see 1 Enoch 1:6-7). The proper behavior for believers at the present moment, therefore, is to wait patiently for the new heavens and new earth characterized by righteousness. They are to live good lives by believing God's promises about the parousia (v. 12). They should lead lives of obedience and faithfulness to God and Jesus, but also to prophets, preachers, yes, and even to the author of this letter! They are to remember the tradition and think correctly about difficult matters such as the day of the parousia (v. 8) or its delay (vv. 9, 15). Thus, they should wait patiently and be prepared (vv. 12, 13, 14) and definitely hold fast (v. 17). By living good lives after this fashion, believers can hasten the day (see Isa 65:17; 66:22; Rev 21:1). This reflects rabbinic thinking that if all Israel kept all the commandments for two successive Sabbaths, the Messiah would come (see Acts 3:19-20).

Today's gospel (Mark 1:1-8) presents the Baptist's preaching and how the listeners are to prepare themselves for the coming of the one mightier than he. The epistle advises believers how to prepare for the return of the Lord. What other advice is needed?

Third Sunday of Advent
1 Thessalonians 5:16-24

This earliest of all the New Testament documents (c. 50 A.D.) is also our introduction to Paul. We meet him and his companions for the first time, approximately 20 years after Paul accepted Jesus as Messiah. Scholars think two letters have been combined into one. (Letter A = 2:13–4:2 written from Athens; and B = 1:1–2:12 and 4:3–5:28 written from Corinth). There is no doubt that today's verses were selected because of the traditional name of this Sunday in Advent: Gaudete Sunday. The staccato character of Paul's concluding exhortations, again a customary part of his letters, has prompted Calvin Roetzel, an eminent American Pauline scholar, to describe this as "shotgun paraenesis." (Paraenesis is exhortations or instructions on how or how not to live.) Christian life ought to be characterized by joy, a fruit of the Spirit (Gal 5:22), and by ceaseless prayer which also proceeds from the Spirit (Rom 8:15-16). Gratitude ("give thanks") is not the same as saying "thank you." In the Middle East, one never says thank you unless one intends to terminate a relationship. "Thank you" means "I won't need you anymore," or "So long, it's been good to know you." That would be equivalent to suicide, since one never knows when one will need a benefactor again. Gratitude in the Middle East is expressed by broadcasting the merits of one's benefactor far and wide, at every opportunity.

5

The exhortation not to quench the Spirit requires special reflection. "Where the Spirit of the Lord is, there is freedom" (2 Cor 3:17). Paul urges the Thessalonians: let freedom prevail! For this to happen, social structure and group control would be reduced to a very low level. If this occurred, it would promote an individualism which neither Paul nor his culture admire. Paul was seriously concerned with good order in the community, group orientation rather than individualism, and edification of all community members. This is very evident in the Corinthian correspondence.

A close look at the verses may help resolve this puzzle. The concluding verses ("May the God of peace . . .") clearly look to a people set apart, a people pure and holy (blameless) in preparation for the advent of the Lord Jesus Messiah. Such people would surely be imbued with the Spirit, and some among them may prophesy. Here, it seems, is the critical point. Quenching the Spirit might result in quenching prophecy. The preferable course of action is to allow freedom but to test everything for authenticity. Retain what is good, discard the rest. Eventually Paul would develop this (in Corinthians) in terms of edification of the community. If it builds up the community, retain it. If freedom destroys the community, it is evil. Refrain from it.

In the gospel (John 1:6-8, 19-28), fellow ethnics had to make a judgment about John the Baptist and his activities. Was this of God and deserving of trust? Or was it a fraud? The passage we read doesn't tell us their conclusion about the Baptist. Paul's exhortations propose one way to decide. Don't squelch the Spirit, don't squelch freedom, but test everything to see whether it builds or destroys community, whether it is life-giving or death-dealing. Judge accordingly.

Fourth Sunday of Advent
Romans 16:25-27

Scholars are nearly unanimous in the opinion that this doxology was added to Paul's epistle at a later date when his letters were gathered together. One reason is the hymnic style that suggests a derivation from liturgical settings. Another reason is the use of the word "mystery" applied to the salvation of non-Israelites ("all nations"), which is characteristic of the Deutero-Paulines, the six letters attributed to Paul but very likely not written by him but after his lifetime (2 Thessalonians, Colossians, Ephesians, 1–2 Timothy, Titus).

"Mystery" refers to God's eternally conceived but hidden plan. Privileged persons in the past (e.g., prophets, visionaries) had access to it through a variety of altered states of consciousness experiences (dreams, trances, visions, and the like, including sky-journeys). The function of such experiences is to comfort and assure believers, especially as they endure trials and tribulations. Specifically in the Deutero-Pauline epistles, the word "mystery" becomes almost a technical term to express what God has accomplished in Jesus (Col 1:26-27; 2:2; Eph 3:3-6, 9). The point in today's verses is that non-Israelites now share in salvation which hitherto had been considered to pertain only to Israel. Of course, this is a point Paul argues in the letter, so the concluding doxology written by another hand after his time serves as an apt conclusion.

The verses also pair well with the gospel (Luke 1:26-38), which reports the angel Gabriel's message to Mary that the son she will conceive and bear will be heir to the throne of David and be called Son of the Most High. Mary's discussion with the angel is an experience that takes place in an altered state of consciousness.

Vigil of the Nativity
Acts 13:16-17, 22-25

Scholars agree that this "sermon" preached by Paul is in reality a Lukan composition following the pattern of earlier sermons (Acts 2:38-40; 3:19-26). Typically there are three parts: God's promise in history (vv. 16-25), the Jesus kerygma as fulfillment of the promise (vv. 26-37), and an exhortation to faith and forgiveness (vv. 38-41). Today's verses present a selective summary of history. God chose our ancestors, among them David, "a man after my own [God's] heart." Jesus, heralded by John, was David's descendant and savior of Israel.

What does it mean to be a person "after God's own heart"? Everything human beings know and say about God is based on human experience. In theological jargon, "all theology is analogy." Further, human experience is culturally shaped. Our non-introspective (actually, anti-introspective!) Mediterranean ancestors in the faith viewed human beings externally as composed of three interacting zones of the body: heart-eyes, mouth-ears, and hands-feet. Heart-eyes symbolized emotion-fused thought, mouth-ears self-expressive speech, and hands-feet purposeful action.

In the New Testament, God too functions in terms of these three zones. Relative to Jesus as son, the Father functions in terms of the heart-eyes zone: God "sees in secret" (Matt 6:18), knows our hearts (Luke 16:15), loves the world (John 3:16), judges each according to his deeds (1 Pet 1:17), and so on. Relative to God, Jesus as Word (mouth-ears zone) reveals the Father (John 1:1ff.). The Father has spoken to us by a Son (Heb 1:12). In relation to the Father, Jesus is the son who reveals the Father. In other words, Jesus is the mouth-ears of God. The hands-feet zone applied to the Father invariably refers to the Spirit who exhibits power, activity, doing, and effectiveness. The "hand of the Lord was upon" many of the prophets (1 Kgs 18:46; 2 Kgs 3:15; etc.). This typical Mediterranean way of viewing the human person may well be the source of the later Christian development of the notion of the Trinity.

Thus, a person "after God's own heart" is one who relates harmoniously with the divine intellect, will, judgment, conscience, personality thrust, core personality—to borrow words from Western cultural perspectives. Such a person is totally pleasing to God. The speech that Luke crafts for Paul draws this phrase from 1 Sam 13:14 where Samuel tells Saul that God has rejected him as king in favor of David. Saul tended to overstep his authority. Too often he took matters into his own hands rather than obey God's law strictly (1 Sam 13:1-15, esp. v. 14; 15:10-33). David was one who would "carry out my [God's] every wish." The gospel for this vigil (Matt 1:18-25) describes the circumstances of the birth of Jesus, one who carried out "God's every wish" even more faithfully than David. In David and Jesus modern believers face a powerful challenge to become people after God's own heart. How does that occur?

Nativity: Midnight Mass
Titus 2:11-14

This letter (along with 1 and 2 Timothy) has been dubbed by tradition as one of the Pastoral epistles. They have been called Pastoral epistles since the eighteenth century because they are addressed to "pastors" of early communities. For this reason, the anonymous person who wrote this letter under the name of Paul, who was already dead, is usually called "the Pastor."

The architects of the lectionary have omitted the first and very important word in today's reading: "for." In Greek this particle always points backwards. The verses that follow this word provide the motive for what preceded (vv. 1-10 are guidelines for behavior based on age and gender: older men/older women; younger men/younger women). Thus have the architects made these verses somewhat "free floating" in the liturgy.

The key word now is "appeared" (v. 11), and its tense in Greek signals a once-and-for-always perspective. How has the grace of God appeared once-and-for-always? The noun "appearance" occurs just six times in the New Testament and always in reference to Jesus. So the process by which God relates to humans (= "grace") has been revealed once and forever in Jesus, in what he said and did and means for us (= salvation).

What is God doing for us? "Training us"; that is, forming us as authentic human beings in all respects: emotionally, intellectually, socially, religiously, politically, and any other way we might imagine. In modern terms, God is relating to us now holistically.

How does God train us? We must (a) reject godless ways and (b) worldly desires. Instead, on the positive side we must live (b') temperately, justly, and (a') devoutly. Notice the arrangement of ideas, so common in the Bible (a, b, b', a'). Godless ways would be equivalent to religious indifferentism or atheistic secularism. If science or some other idol usurps God's role to be in charge of life, the result is a godless way of life.

Worldly desires might be interpreted as accepting the dictates of one's culture without critical evaluation. Many people in Western culture derive a sense of self-worth from having a job or the right kind of job. Does human worth and identity depend on a job, or on something other than one's job? Instead, believers are called to lead sensible, self-controlled lives and to live justly or uprightly. This means one must live in good interpersonal relationships with other human beings. Finally, to live devoutly is to acknowledge God's reign in our personal lives. While this may sound like excessive reliance upon personal efforts, the Pastor says exactly the opposite: it is God's grace that makes good living possible. God's activity on our behalf through Jesus makes us true human beings. Moreover, God's training is effective because of Jesus' voluntary death in total obedience to the Father so that we might be cleansed and eager to do good.

This reflection on the consequences of Jesus' life and death for us is a fitting transition to the gospel (Luke 2:1-14), which announces the birth of Jesus. Clearly the feast is about much more than the joy, lights, and gifts so characteristic of the season.

Nativity: Mass at Dawn
Titus 3:4-7

Scholars recognize these verses as a popular "creed" which the Pastor inserted at this point in his letter as a comment on good deeds (3:1, 5, 8) and bad deeds (3:9). (Examples of other such creedal statements in the Pastorals would be 1 Tim 1:15; 2:4-6; 3:16; 6:12-16; 2 Tim 1:8-10; Titus 2:11-14.) Such creedal statements may have originated in the context of liturgies. If so, the Pastor's ready reliance on creeds in his instructions about proper behavior (good and bad deeds) is an excellent example of moving from liturgy to life among our ancestors in the faith.

The Pastor's creed-based observation is that good deeds by themselves don't merit anything from God (v. 5). Rather, everything is a free gift coming to us through baptism. But remember that in Mediterranean culture, there really are no free gifts. Every gift expects one in return, or at least some response. This response is "good deeds."

Once again, these verses seem well suited to the gospel (Luke 2:15-20) in which the shepherds who received word of the birth of Jesus don't just put it on their calendars or their lists of things "to do," but rather immediately (so typical of the Mediterranean culture's intense focus on the present) go to Bethlehem, see for themselves, and return glorifying and praising God. Would you consider yourself a person who acts promptly on a resolution or one who procrastinates? Would it make a difference?

Nativity: Mass during the Day
Hebrews 1:1-6

Writing in the name of Paul sometime between A.D. 60 and 100, this anonymous author has produced a masterpiece of literature and theological reflection about Jesus. These opening verses sum up the essay and the significance of today's feast: Jesus is Son and word of God, God's definitive self-disclosure. They are also very different in form and content from the customary opening verses of Paul's letters.

The final verses (4-6) emphasize that Jesus is superior to the angels. Indeed he is an agent of revelation far superior to the angels. (For angels as agents or mediators of revelation see 1 Kgs 13:18; Isaiah 6; Daniel 7–12; 2 Esdras 3–14.) Since the author does not engage in specific polemics, scholars have been unable to determine the reason for this emphasis upon Jesus as superior to the angels. Some scholars think this community may have been attracted to or participated in worshiping angels. The letter provides no evidence for this hypothesis. What is more likely is that the community may have thought they were worshiping with angels (e.g., Isa 6:3). This is a familiar idea in first-century Judaism which later became an element of Christian liturgical practice. Variations on the phrase "And so, with all the choirs of angels in heaven we proclaim your glory" appear in prefaces throughout the Liturgical Year. If the author thought that associating Jesus with the angels in some way minimized Jesus' role as mediator, it is surprising that he does not dwell upon it more explicitly.

The author's purpose is clear. He seeks to reinforce the sublime dimension of Jesus' exalted status which guarantees salvation to believers. This strong statement prepares the way for his subsequent presentation of Jesus' humiliation which gained that salvation for his followers.

This reading links well with the gospel (John 1:1-18), which is the classic statement of Jesus' exalted status in the New Testament. It also looks back to the gospel for the Mass at Dawn, which highlighted a special function for angels at the birth of Jesus. Given the popularity of angels in the contemporary world, Hebrews invites modern believers to examine their faith and make certain that Jesus remains central and unsurpassed as our mediator with the Father.

Sunday within the Octave of Christmas: Holy Family Sunday
Hebrews 11:8, 11-12, 17-19

The whole of Hebrews 11 is a carefully constructed unit reflecting on faith (see the inclusio or inclusion formed in vv. 1-2 and 39-40 by the notion of receiving witness through faith). It begins with a definition of faith (vv. 1-2) and then reviews biblical heroes who illustrate his notion of faith. Today's verses focus on Sarah the Matriarch and Abraham the Patriarch.

The sacred author understands faith to have two dimensions: it relates to the attainment of hoped-for goals and to the perception of invisible realities. It is the latter that supports a believer in trials and tribulations which test one's faith, or as the Mediterranean world would understand it, one's loyalty. What are some of the invisible realities (things not seen) that motivate a believer to remain faithful and loyal? Of course, it is God ("the one who is invisible" 11:27), God's existence and providence (11:6), trustworthiness (11:11), and power (11:19).

The story of Abraham as a model of faith is presented in three sections: his election, migration, and reception of the promised child (vv. 8-12); Abraham as a sojourner (vv. 13-16); and the binding of Isaac (vv. 17-22). In the first section (vv. 8-12), the sacred author of Hebrews stretches his sources, as is common in retelling biblical traditions. Verses 10 and 11 attribute motivations to the characters which do not appear in the original account and are implausible in that original context. But for the sacred author, this introduces his reflective comments in the next four verses (vv. 13-16). So faith, sticking with God no matter what, motivates Abraham to obey and to endure while patiently waiting to achieve the promised goal. One ought not press the biological comments in vv. 11 and 12. The real focus is the birth of Isaac, the child of promise. Life can come from death through faith.

The second segment praises the loyalty of the patriarchs who were seeking not an earthly but a heavenly homeland. It interrupts the reflection on Abraham. Clearly this reflection is for the benefit of the sacred author's audience, fellow believers in Jesus. Their faith has caused alienation from family and home and rendered them sojourners, subject to the suffering that accompanies alien status.

The final segment resumes the story of Abraham with his willingness to sacrifice his son who was the foundation of the fulfillment of God's promises. Again the sacred author restates the motif that God can bring life from death.

Today's gospel (Luke 2:22-40) presents Simeon and Anna as two models of loyalty to God who like Abraham attained the fulfillment of a long-awaited dream. Given the tendency in Western culture to form pragmatic friendships, what can modern Western believers do to strengthen their loyalties (= faith)?

January 1:
Octave Day of Christmas: Solemnity of the Blessed Virgin Mary, The Mother of God
Galatians 4:4-7

For Paul, the advent of Jesus marked the beginning of a new "time." Specifically, it was the redemptive death of Jesus that formed the dividing line signaling the end of one age and the beginning of another (then–now; once–but now). Jesus was born an Israelite and circumcised, hence he became subject to the law (then). But his death abrogated the covenant of law and established a new covenant of faith and grace (now; Gal 3:13-14). In his own life, Jesus manifests the precise pattern of the covenant of faith, its significance, and how it works in day-to-day life. Jesus is the unique "son" that God promised to Abraham (Gal 3:16), thus becoming a model for whoever would be son (or daughter) with God (Gal 4:5-7). This defines the status of any and every believer. Just as Jesus prayed to his Abba (Mark 14:36, the only place this word appears in the Gospels), so his followers are filled with the Spirit and pray as he did: "Abba, Father" (Gal 4:6).

It is probably unnecessary but still helpful to remind ourselves that the Aramaic word "Abba" never meant "Daddy," but rather exactly as reported in the Greek of Mark meant and was understood as "Father." Even in the English language, there is a difference between "Father" and "Daddy." In 1988, James Barr reviewed the linguistic evidence and noted that in its cultural context, that is, the ancient Israelite social system, Abba was a term of formal address. It was not used as a familiar, intimate, warm, and loving term. The significance for these passages (Mark and Galatians) is that now after the death of Jesus, his followers have the same relationship to God that he had. That is indeed good news. The term, however, fits well into the Mediterranean cultural matrix where love for the father is always demonstrated in a respectful way. In this culture, the son is not the father's equal or pal. As reflected in Sirach (3:6-7), the culture notes that "he who fears the LORD honors his father, and serves his parents as rulers."

Luke (2:16-21) depicts the way in which Jesus was indeed subject to his parents from the very beginning. He was circumcised on the eighth day and given the name assigned by the angel. The pattern of his life lived faithfully under the law helps to appreciate the new relationship with God that Jesus made possible for all, Israelite and non-Israelites alike.

Second Sunday after Christmas
Ephesians 1:3-6, 15-18

Contemporary scholarly opinion lists this letter among the
Deutero-Paulines. It was likely written after Paul's death by
disciples sometime between 80–100 A.D. These verses are part
of the customary blessing (vv. 3-14) and thanksgiving (vv. 15-
23) sections which begin most of the letters. Why should we
bless God? Primarily because God chose us in Jesus just as
God chose special people before us (see Deut 14:2). Given
the gratuitous nature of the choice, one can only marvel and
be grateful. Of course, that election involves an obligation:
God's chosen people must be holy and without blemish in
God's presence. Yet another reason for requiring such holiness and purity is the Ephesian congregation's conviction
that it too, perhaps like the Colossians, was convinced that
angels were in the midst of the worshiping community (see
Eph 3:10; also 2:6). This is similar to the sentiments at Qumran where anyone physically blemished "shall not enter to
take their place among the congregation of famous men, for
the angels of holiness are among their congregation" (1QSa
2:8-9).

God has not just chosen us but rather adopted us. Scholars observe that in this culture where family (kinship) is one
of the dominant social institutions and is rather extensive
and complex, there was no mechanism for adoption. That
Paul would reach such a conclusion would be an interesting
breakthrough. Those who heard this from Paul and his circle

would be awed. God's election bestows incredible honor and far-reaching consequences.

The thanksgiving section (vv. 15-18) appears to have been patterned after Phlm 4-5. Paul prays that they may receive wisdom and revelation in order that they may come to know God even better. Wisdom in the Bible involves practical or experiential knowledge and the ability to choose proper conduct. In Paul, wisdom often involved understanding more clearly God's activity in Jesus and the benefits believers receive from such knowledge. The upshot of Paul's prayer is that the Ephesians might appreciate the immense privileges that God has bestowed upon them.

The gospel for today (John 1:1-18) talks about the Word who literally in Greek "pitched his tent among us" (v. 14). Those who received him were empowered to become "children of God" (v. 12). The Ephesian verses provide still further information about the truly blessed condition of being adopted by God. No doubt all modern believers can readily echo Paul's prayer that they, too, might understand and appreciate the astounding honor of being so chosen by God. How amazing is this God!

January 6: Epiphany
Ephesians 3:2-3a, 5-6

[For brief background, see Fifteenth Sunday in Ordinary Time.] The author of Ephesians repeats Paul's great insight here, that non-Israelites (Gentiles) have full and co-equal membership with Israelites in the Church through Christ Jesus. In the Greek texts three adjectives with the prefix syn- (together) make this point emphatically (co-heirs, co-members, co-partners, v. 6). Actually, the insight results from a direct revelation from God (compare Gal 1:12, 16) which by this time in the tradition has become normative. Given the history of the chosen people, the covenant, and related concepts, only God could have revealed that the divine will now include non-Israelites in that people. This idea would be too preposterous for any human being to initiate on personal initiative.

Another interesting point is that this revelation/insight has been given to "holy apostles and prophets" (v. 5). Scholars remind us that Paul (e.g., in Galatians 1–2) insisted that he alone received the distinctive revelation concerning the place of non-Israelites in the Church. That the author of Ephesians now extends it to others (apostles and prophets) is a strong argument that this is an author writing in the name of Paul, and not Paul himself.

The common link between this reading and the gospel for today's feast (Matt 2:1-12) is the Magi, non-Israelites who come to do homage to Jesus at his birth. In Romans, Paul makes the boldest statement of his understanding of the relationship of non-Israelites to Israelites by calling the grafting of non-Israelites to Israelites "unnatural" or "contrary to nature" (Rom 11:24). Only a revelation from God could convince humans that this is the divine will. Contemporary Church members who are overwhelmingly of non-Israelite lineage should be awed by God's decision. Today's feast provides an opportunity to formulate a convincing reply to a question frequently asked by outsiders: "Knowing the history of the Church and its warts, why do you remain a Christian?"

Baptism of the Lord
(First Sunday in Ordinary Time)
1 John 5:1-9

[For background to 1 John see Second Sunday of Easter.] The first four verses of today's reading focus on love, hence continue the author's attack upon the Secessionists. These claim to love, but in the sacred author's view, they lie. His argument is: everyone who believes Jesus is the Messiah is a child of God. Of course, the Secessionists believed this, as did the Johannine community. The author continues: every one who loves the parent loves the child (his argument is generic; there is no reason for translating father with an upper case letter). Conversely, loving the children is a way of loving the parent. So if the Secessionists do not love Johannine believers, they cannot really love God. And if they say they love members of their group, well they are not children of God because their faith is imperfect, hence they have no brothers to love. Further, the Secessionists claim to love God but do not emphasize keeping the commandments. But true love is obedient love, and obedient the Secessionists are not. Lest his own followers get discouraged and submit to pressures from the Secessionists, the author reminds them that commandments (proper behavior) are not burdensome for true children of God.

Johannine scholars acknowledge that vv. 5-9 are very obscure and difficult to interpret. This is a splendid example of high context writing. Surely the letter recipients could read between the lines and supply what the author was presupposing. The Secessionists apparently said that Jesus was the Messiah, the Son of God, who became such when he "came by water," as revealed by the Spirit. The author of 1 John broadens this by alluding to the crucifixion of Jesus and the flow of blood and water from his side (John 19:34). The flowing blood was proper according to the Torah so that it could be sprinkled, and the water is not water of baptism (as the Secessionists would claim) but the water that flowed with the blood. The testimony of the Beloved Disciple to this event continues in the tradition of the Johannine Community. The Spirit is still bearing witness.

The significance of witnesses derives from Deut 19:15 which requires two or three. Throughout the gospel of John, multiple witnesses are cited (John 8:18; 5:31-40). This was a technique used by the Johannine community in their arguments with fellow Israelites concerning the divinity of Jesus. Here the author summons it in his debate with the Secessionists over the humanity of Jesus. The Secessionists point to the witness of the Baptist testifying that the incarnation alone is sufficient. The author of 1 John summons three: Spirit, water, blood. How? On a symbolic level, the reference is to sacramental actions familiar to the Johannine Community: Spirit = anointing (see 2 John 2:20, 27); water = baptism (John 3:5); blood = Eucharist (John 6:51-58). Sacraments bear witness to the saving nature of Jesus' death: they constitute people as children of God, nourish them with heavenly food and drink, and they are actions by which true believers share in the act by which Jesus conquered the world (John 16:33).

By pairing this reading with the Baptism of Jesus reported today by Mark (1:7-11), one can see event and interpretation. Believers too focused on getting at the facts (e.g., in Jesus' life) may miss the point of what the facts mean, and how that meaning made sense out of the lives of subsequent believers. The readings for today's feast offer an opportunity to reflect on events and their interpretation.

Second Sunday in Ordinary Time
1 Corinthians 6:13c-15a, 17-20

This letter was probably written from Ephesus about the year 54 A.D. The broader context of these verses clarify Paul's intentions. Paul and the Corinthians held contrasting views of the human body. For Paul, believers were to safeguard the integrity and holiness of the physical body. They were to control the body and its orifices (mouth, genitals) through which it could be polluted. For his opponents, the physical body was an organism that needed no control. For them, freedom that comes with redemption by Jesus encourages spontaneity and rejects controlling rules and laws. This explains their contrasting ideas about fornication considered in today's verses.

Second, the Corinthians summarized their views in slogans: "all things are lawful for me" (1 Cor 6:12); "Food for the stomach and the stomach for food" (it makes no difference what one eats—6:13). The New American Bible translation puts these in quotation marks since Paul is quoting his opponents. A third slogan, "Every sin a person commits is outside the body" (only intentions count—6:18), is not in quotation marks because Paul reinterprets it in his critical response. "Every other sin . . . is outside the body; but sexual sins which involve crossing body boundaries and penetrating bodily orifices takes place within the physical body."

Paul's opponents have moved in the direction of individualism similar to that familiar to members of modern Western cultures. Paul and his thinking remain anchored in the Mediterranean cultural concept of dyadic individualism and collectivistic personality. In this view, the individual must always be subordinate to and responsible for the well-being of the group, the community. Thus, in Paul's thinking individual believers with their physical bodies constitute the community which is Christ ("your bodies are members of Christ"). This community is where the Holy Spirit resides; the community ("your body") is a Temple of the Holy Spirit. The community therefore must be holy. Individual members are obliged to see to that.

But if individual believers join their physical bodies in illicit sexual liaisons, they pollute the community which is Christ. Paul's adamant conclusion: you are not your own (to do as you please, like an individualist). You must honor God in your physical body to ensure that the social body will remain holy. This thinking fits perfectly well with the Mediterranean cultural concept of collectivistic personality.

In the gospel (John 1:35-42), Jesus calls his first disciples. The first two come from among the Baptist's disciples. If these disciples are like their master, they are worthy persons. Then one of these, Andrew, calls his brother Simon. If Andrew was worthy, Simon his blood-kin is also worthy. Perhaps this explains why the invitations give no requirements for discipleship other than responding to the invitation. In contrast, Paul reminds believers that they "have been purchased at a price" in order to become members of the community. From this perspective of collectivistic personalities, Paul lays out some strict regulations for believers about the integrity of the physical body which has an impact on the social body, the community. How does the behavior of modern, individualist believers with relationship to their physical bodies bless or taint the community? Or does it matter to individualists at all?

Third Sunday in Ordinary Time
1 Corinthians 7:29-31

In general, Mediterranean culture's primary temporal orientation is to the present moment rather broadly understood; it includes tomorrow as well. In antiquity, the concept of a distant future was practically non-existent. The closest they came to the notion of a future is better expressed as forthcoming. A harvest is forthcoming from seeds already planted. A baby is certainly forthcoming from a woman already pregnant. Since Jesus died and has already been raised, his return is already forthcoming. Paul and his contemporaries believed it was imminent (1 Thess 4:16-17; 1 Cor 15:51-52). Paul was firmly convinced he would still be alive when Jesus returned. It was only close encounters with death (e.g., 2 Cor 1:8) that brought Paul and his contemporaries (e.g., 1 Thess 4:13) to the realization that the Second Coming of Jesus might be delayed for a very long time. Still, the prevailing orientation of this culture to the present moment explains the urgency of Paul's exhortations: "The time is running out."

In that context, the general meaning of his practical advice is: "don't get wrapped up in anything that would prevent you from being fully prepared." If you are married, this is hardly the time to start a family. If you have purchased land, don't bother preparing it either for a building or for farming. Time is running out.

In the Gospel (Mark 1:14-20), Jesus preaches with similar urgency: "This is the time of fulfillment. The kingdom of God is at hand. Repent, and believe in the gospel" (1:15). When Simon, Andrew, James, and John hear Jesus' call, they follow immediately. The American proverb: "Don't put off for tomorrow things you can do today" suggests that we have a tendency precisely to delay resolute action to another time, to tomorrow. What ought believers do today in order to be fully prepared for the eventualities the Scriptures describe for us?

Fourth Sunday in Ordinary Time
1 Corinthians 7:32-35

Key to understanding Paul's thoughts on marriage as expressed in these verses is an appreciation for a cardinal Mediterranean value: limited good. This value consists in the firm belief that all goods in life are finite in quantity and already distributed: honor, semen, beauty, health, wealth, land, reputation, etc. Loyalty is one of these limited goods. There is no more where this came from. There is only so much to go around. The one who can give all her or his loyalty to a single person gives more loyalty than the one who has to divide her or his loyalty between two or more persons. Hence, the married person has divided loyalties; the unmarried person can give all her or his loyalty to God.

Murphy-O'Connor observes that while Paul has no qualms imposing administrative decisions, he shows restraint in imposing moral judgments. In v. 35 Paul concludes his comments by saying: "I am telling you this for your own benefit, not to impose a restraint upon you." In other words, take it or leave it, but strive to adhere to the Lord without distraction.

Western culture, in contrast, believes in unlimited or limitless goods: there is always more where this came from. Western citizens can be loyal to their family, their occupation, their hobbies, etc. For the Western citizen, time rather than loyalty appears to be the more dominant concern. Hence Westerners have invented quality time which can be of brief duration but very intense and filled with meaning.

The gospel for today (Mark 1:21-28) illustrates the consequences of Jesus' loyalty to God. He teaches with authority and has mastery over unclean spirits. Both readings present an opportunity for modern believers, whether married or not, to review their loyalties. No matter what one's station in life, divided loyalties in our culture are possible, acceptable, and often necessary. How do we maintain and balance them?

Fifth Sunday in Ordinary Time
1 Corinthians 9:16-19, 22-23

There are no free gifts in the Mediterranean world. Every gift carries the expectation of a gift in return. The principle of limited goods (my gift to you depletes my goods) joins with the cultural practice of dyadic contract (your gift requires that I reciprocate so that your supply of goods may be complete again). It was on this basis that Jesus sent his disciples to preach the gospel (Mark 6:8-12). Preachers can expect support from the community. If it is not offered, preachers must move on. In these verses, however, Paul insists that he is preaching to the Corinthians "free of charge" (v. 18). Actually, the Macedonians are supporting Paul at this time (2 Cor 11:7-9), so the preaching isn't exactly free.

Paul's main point, however, is that he tempers his freedom with self-discipline: "I have made myself a slave to all" (v. 22). Thus, though he has a right based on the words of Jesus to expect support for his preaching, he forgoes the right for the sake of the common good. He restrains his legitimate freedom in order to keep the community whole and holy. Here is yet another glowing example of the Mediterranean collectivistic personality subordinating individual preferences to the good of the social body. According to Paul, Christian freedom is not license but rather an obligation to serve each other through love (Gal 5:13-15). He consistently gives personal witness to this in his pastoral practice.

In the gospel for today (Mark 1:29-39) we see another example of dyadic contract. Jesus heals Peter's mother-in-law, who responds by waiting on him and his entourage. "You do me a favor; I owe you a favor and do one in return." But going beyond that, Jesus went to the nearby villages to preach and drive out demons. His movement made it impossible for the beneficiaries to repay him personally. The hope was that through love they would serve one another in their needs. The readings invite modern believers to reflect upon freedom, that value so highly cherished in the West. Is it readily sacrificed for the common good, or is freedom proclaimed even to the detriment of others?

Sixth Sunday in Ordinary Time
1 Corinthians 10:31–11:1

"Be imitators of me, as I am of Christ" (1 Cor 10:31). Is this bluster, arrogance, or honesty? Because he repeats it so often (1 Thess 1:6; 2:14; Gal 4:2; Phil 3:17; 4:9; 1 Cor 4:16) to communities that knew him personally, Paul is probably giving his honest self-appraisal. These are clear claims to honor. No one in this culture would make this kind of claim if it could be denied. The shame would be too great and too costly.

The claim is not preposterous. Since Jesus is no longer physically visible in this community, his followers must mirror "the life of Jesus" (2 Cor 4:10) for others to learn and imitate. In what way did Paul think he was worthy of imitation? Chiefly by behaving in such a way that God would be honored. This is the general truth of his statement. Specifically in this instance, however, the behavior to imitate is not to put stumbling blocks in the way of those (Judeans, non-Judeans, or the *ekklesia*) who want to draw near to Jesus. Since he mentions eating and drinking, the stumbling blocks might entail practices that could be viewed as belittling or denying the value of food regulations such as Leviticus 12. While Jesus and his followers believed God had changed these (see Acts 10; compare Mark 7:19), their liberated behaviors could prove offensive and off-putting to those who did not share this belief. Paul's idea was to "save" these people rather than repulse them.

In today's gospel (Mark 1:40-45), Jesus breaks purity rules by touching the man afflicted with a skin condition negatively evaluated by Leviticus 13–14 in order to restore meaning to his life (to heal him). Paul, too, is concerned with bringing new meaning to life to all who are attracted to Jesus. Paul, however, seems to manifest greater sensitivity by warning against setting up stumbling blocks, perhaps by blatantly insisting on one's liberated views to the hurt of others. The strategies are worth pondering: full-steam ahead with liberating ideas? or sensitive respect for others who do not yet feel so liberated?

Seventh Sunday in Ordinary Time
2 Corinthians 1:18-22

The background to Paul's second letter to the Corinthians is that disunity and other problems noted in the first letter seem to have worsened. To complicate matters, Paul broke his promise to visit them (1 Cor 16:5), and his opponents in Corinth used that to claim that Paul could not be trusted. Perhaps his preaching too should be doubted.

Today's verses are a theological digression which is rooted in a peculiar Middle Eastern cultural trait. Because honor is the core cultural value, no one ever wants to cause shame to self or others. If you ask me a question, and I don't know the answer, I will give you one anyway. It is imperative for me not to admit I don't know the answer, for that would shame me. The challenge to you is to evaluate my answer as reliable or unreliable. Or if I know you are seeking a certain kind of information, I will give it to you. I will always say what you want to hear. The son in Jesus' parable who told his father he would go work in the vineyard when he had no intention of so doing at all acted very honorably (Matt 21:28ff.). He said what his father wanted to hear, thus honoring his father rather than shaming him as the brother did.

Because he broke his promise to visit them, Paul's Corinthian enemies accuse him of saying what people want to hear though he probably had no intention of visiting them at all. Paul defends himself as trustworthy because he preaches the sure and reliable gospel of a faithful and trustworthy God and the totally committed and faithful son, Jesus Messiah. God would not have selected an unreliable minister to preach the sure gospel. All God's promises were realized in Jesus: seed of Abraham (Gal 3:16), Davidic Messiah (Rom 1:4), the last Adam (1 Cor 15:45), and more. Our Amen joins with the Son's agreement to fulfill the faithful Father's promises. Believers are visibly marked (his seal upon us) as belonging to the Messiah Jesus. They also have received the Spirit as a down payment, a guarantee that the promises will be fulfilled.

In today's gospel (Mark 1:1-12), Jesus is moved by the steadfast loyalty of those who brought the paralytic to him for healing. This is the kind of loyalty Paul sees in God and which Paul insists that he too possesses. Modern believers tend to give the word "faith" an intellectual content. Translating this Middle Eastern cultural concept more fittingly as loyalty or unswerving fidelity offers a new consideration.

Eighth Sunday in Ordinary Time
2 Corinthians 3:1b-6

Middle Eastern culture is basically agonistic or combative. This means it tends toward confrontation and conflict. Any one who reads Paul's letters, especially the Corinthian correspondence, can see this trait quite clearly. In these verses, Paul is defending himself once again against attacks by his opponents. They claim he has recommended himself (e.g., see 1 Thess 2:1-12). In contrast, they point with pride that they have been commissioned and sent by another congregation, perhaps Jerusalem.

One example of a letter of recommendation is Rom 16:1-2. It isn't very long, but the authority of the sender (Paul) makes it easier for Phoebe to receive hospitality from that community which does not know her and which she has never visited before. In general in Middle Eastern culture, foreigners or strangers are suspected of being up to no good. Travel is deviant, and once one has gone beyond one's home village, a letter of recommendation or gracious hospitality is necessary to guarantee safe passage. Paul says the Corinthian community in which he ministered is his letter of recommendation; they assure the legitimacy of his apostleship (see 1 Cor 9:2). [It seems preferable to read "written in your hearts" rather than "our" hearts which doesn't seem to make sense, even though it is supported by better manuscript evidence.] Such a letter—that is, the existence of this community—is a letter of recommendation from Jesus himself.

God makes it possible for Paul to accomplish his ministry of a new covenant. Paul then distinguishes two views of the new covenant: his opponents' view which insisted on the law (letter), and his view which emphasizes the spirit. The law (letter) is death dealing, but the Spirit is life-giving.

Another conflict is reflected in the gospel (Mark 2:18-22) on the topic of fasting. Jesus' reflections on old and new are comparable to Paul's reflections on the difference between himself and his opponents. Westerners are generally reluctant to give offense, hence they tend to gloss over differences politely. Is there an advantage to the conflicts that characterize agonistic cultures?

Ninth Sunday
in Ordinary Time
2 Corinthians 4:6-11

Four times in the Corinthian letters Paul mentions his hardships (1 Cor 4:8-13; 2 Cor 4:7-12; 6:3-10; 11:23-30). These passages raise two questions. What kind of a person dwells on suffering? And whence come these sufferings? In our culture, we frown on people who recount their suffering, especially if it is done in detail. One reason for this attitude is that we believe all human beings can be in charge of their lives and do something about suffering whatever its source. The Middle Eastern cultural belief was that human beings are not at all in control of their existence, and the best they can do is endure heroically whatever suffering comes their way. Those who would hear Paul's report of his sufferings and how he endures them would applaud him as a male who has been so well socialized into his role that he can serve as a role model to others. This is certainly one of Paul's purposes here. He is not a masochist; he is a type of cultural hero.

Whence come these sufferings? Like everyone else in his agonistic culture, Paul perceived himself as living in and indeed experiencing a hostile world that was out to harm and ruin him. We really cannot trust anyone outside of our families. The hostile forces could be evil men or evil spirits. No matter, the point is that these sufferings are undeserved and therefore unjust.

But Paul is more than a cultural hero. He points to the distinctive nature of suffering by a believer. Paul's life (his practice) conforms to his preaching (Christ and him crucified). It is God's plan that believers will be tested and worn down by suffering so as to manifest the life of Jesus in the body. What should emerge from this is that the life of Jesus, authentic human existence, might become all the more clearly manifest.

Mark (2:23–3:6) notes that Jesus' opponents were so piqued by his blatant violations of the Sabbath (which nevertheless brought renewed life to those in need of it) that they colluded with the Herodians to put Jesus to death. Ironically, the death of Jesus resulted in new life for those who believe in him. Paul sees his own life experiences testifying to this new life in his ministry. How can modern believers bear witness to new life that derives from suffering, often unjust and undeserved? What would be some examples?

Tenth Sunday in Ordinary Time
2 Corinthians 4:13–5:1

The composite picture that Paul presents of himself through-out his letters is curious. He boasts that he does not allow the local Corinthian church to support him and thereby play the role of "friends" in his life (1 Cor 9:4-12; 2 Cor 11:7-9; he did, however, allow this in Philippi, 4:15-19). Some schol-ars believe this is part of Paul's crisis at Corinth. He refused to accept patronage and the lower status into which that would place him, that of a client. The reason for this is that Paul wanted to be viewed as a broker who puts clients in contact with God. A broker has no clients, no one has to be beholden to a broker.

In today's verses, Paul demonstrates how he faces death without fear. Though externally he appears to be a wreck (per-haps even physically), his inner self is being renewed day by day. He is absolutely confident that the one who raised Jesus will raise him also. If his physical life should end, he will have a new existence with God in heaven. Everything he does is for the benefit of the community, so that, as the community grows, increasing numbers can give glory and thanks to God.

The gospel for today (Mark 3:20-35) recounts growing hostility to Jesus and alienation from his family, high prices to pay for conviction and single-minded devotion to God. Paul's sentiments also reflect the high price he paid for single-minded devotion to his ministry as willed by God. What price does the modern believer risk paying for steadfast loy-alty to God?

First Sunday of Lent
1 Peter 3:18-22

Commenting on this passage, Martin Luther said: "This is a strange text and certainly a more obscure passage than any other passage in the New Testament. I still do not know what for sure the apostle means." (*Luther's Works,* vol. 30, p. 113). Contemporary scholars can offer significant insight.

The verses seem to be a conflation of two traditions: a hymn or creed (3:18, 22) and a catechetical section on baptism (3:19-21). To understand these high-context verses it is important to be familiar with Gen 6:1-2 and its interpretation in Enoch. The sacred authors of 1 Peter continue their exhortation to believers to remain faithful. According to Israelite tradition (Gen 6:1-2), angelic sinners instigated the "original sin" of human beings (which was punished by the flood). These lustful beings impregnated human women who gave birth to giants. The beings were eternally imprisoned by God, but they continued to induce human beings to sin. Again according to tradition in 1 Enoch, God took this righteous man to himself (Gen 5:21-24) and Enoch had visions. In his altered states of consciousness experiences, Enoch ascended through a series of heavens where he announced to the angelic spirits that they would be imprisoned there (1 Enoch 12–21) because of their wickedness (1 Enoch 6–11).

The sacred authors of 1 Peter (Silvanus, 5:12, and Mark, 5:13, but likely not Peter, 1:1, who was already dead) present the Risen Jesus as another Enoch who as he was raised to life (v. 18) ascended through the sky to be exalted at God's right hand (v. 22). On his way, he announced to these angels, authorities, and powers that they remained condemned and would be subordinated to him.

Likewise as God once saved Noah and his family (eight is a symbol of resurrection; see Justin, *Dial.* 138:1-2), so now in the present is God saving these strangers and resident aliens in Asia Minor through the deluge of their baptism. Thus baptism, which gives believers new life initiated by the resurrection of Jesus, now saves believers by fostering loyal obedience to God's will (see 2:19; 3:16).

Jesus' successful passing of the test of his loyalty as beloved Son in today's gospel (Mark 1:12-15) is a fitting partner to the verses in 1 Peter which assure believers that they can be as successful as Jesus in remaining steadfast when their loyalty to God is tested.

Second Sunday of Lent
Romans 8:31b-34

Paul wrote this letter from Corinth, or Cenchrae, its port, around 57–58 A.D. This text-segment brings to a conclusion Romans 5–8 in which Paul has described the Christian experience of new life at peace with God, thanks to God's love. These hymn-like verses celebrate the reality of the good things God has determined for the elect. Realizing this, what else can one say except: "If God is for us, who can be against us?" Reference to God not sparing his own Son alludes to Abraham not sparing Isaac (the first reading in today's liturgy) and echoes Jesus' reminder of his destiny to his chosen disciples on the way down from the mountain after their altered state of consciousness experience of the true identity of Jesus. Notice Paul's not too subtle reference to the death of the Son "for us ALL," indicating that non-Israelites were included also, fulfilling the inclusive promise to Abraham (Rom 4:16). Further, if God didn't back down on this gift, how could God retract "everything else"?

The second question: "Who will bring a charge against God's chosen ones?" derives from a forensic setting and draws inspiration from Isa 50:8-9a. The allusion is to an accusing angel, but given that God has already acquitted us, what lesser being could level a charge at the final judgment that would stick? Moreover, God's Messiah, who is at the right hand of God, continues to intercede for us "as brother" (Rom 8:29). Such privileged kinship makes us invincible against any final threat.

Third Sunday of Lent
1 Corinthians 1:22-25

The ancient world was intrigued by paradox and reversal. Imagine efforts to save life that end up losing it, but losing life ends up saving it (Mark 8:35). Reversal is at the center of Paul's argument in these verses. Basing themselves on Genesis 1 and their experience of a well ordered and predictable Temple system, Israelites concluded that God behaved in orderly and predictable ways. They could expect constancy and fairness in life. Non-Israelites (Gentiles) relied on logic, rational speculation, and drew a similar conclusion: life is predictable.

These verses center on the generally agreed upon map of honorable persons shared by all in the ancient Middle Eastern world. A person who died by crucifixion had no place on this map. Crucifixion is a shameful death reserved for criminals and not for honorable citizens. A crucified Messiah is indeed a stumbling block to Israelites. It was not what they expected. It is also a stumbling block to non-Israelites in this cultural world because crucifixion is patently dishonorable, outright shameful. Paul, however, insists that in this matter God engages in reversal, for in God's view, Christ crucified is truly "the power of God and the Wisdom of God" (v. 24). God is perfectly free to act in ways that totally contradict the patterns of order and honor commonly accepted in any culture, even the patterns to which observant Israelites have long been socialized. In other words, God is always free to draw new maps of value, of honor that deliberately reverse the expected pattern that would obtain divine favor.

In today's gospel (John 2:13-25), Jesus causes a disturbance in the Temple to call attention to what he believes is a perversion of its purpose and function. Another link between the epistle and gospel is the dubious value of "signs." Both Paul and John indicate that people who seek signs manifest a refusal to trust God. Perhaps this signals a satisfaction with the status quo. If we let God be God, we will surely be in for a surprise.

Fourth Sunday of Lent
Ephesians 2:4-10

[For brief background, see Fifteenth Sunday in Ordinary Time.] Like others in his culture, Paul divides time into "before" and "after" periods with variations: then vs. now (Eph 2:11-22; 5:8); once but now (Eph 2:1-10); mystery hidden vs. mystery now revealed (Eph 3:4-7, 8-11); and mystery promised vs. mystery now given (2 Tim 1:9-11). Here the one who writes this letter in the name of Paul describes the Ephesians' conditions as once being dead (in their transgressions), but now alive with Christ. More than being raised to new life, believers have been enthroned with Jesus in the sky. However, there is a variation here. Whereas Paul ordinarily contrasts faith and good works (e.g., Rom 3:28), this letter writer contrasts God's mercy, love, grace with good works. In today's gospel (John 3:14-21), John's Jesus spells out God's love and gift of life eternal to those who believe in him.

Fifth Sunday of Lent
Hebrews 5:7-9

[For the context of these verses see Thirtieth Sunday in Ordinary Time.] Today's verses explain how Jesus in his earthly life demonstrated his full solidarity with human beings in his concrete cultural setting. To appreciate the sacred author's point, let us review the process by which young boys were raised from infancy to puberty. [Review Twenty-Eighth Sunday in Ordinary Time.] A wife was not fully integrated into her husband's family until she bore a son (cf. 1 Sam 1:1-19). The birth of a son was great joy for all. Boys were raised by all the women with little to no male presence until the age of puberty. They were pampered, pleasured, and in modern terms quite "spoiled." Lacking male role-models during this time of life, they entered puberty with a sense of gender-ambiguity. At puberty, without the assistance of a rite of passage (bar mitzvah is Talmudic in origin), boys were pushed unceremoniously into the harsh and hierarchical world of men. They ran back to the comforts of the women's world, but the women would simply return them to the men's world.

Proverbs (e.g., 13:24; 23:13) and Sirach (30:1, 12) prescribe frequent and severe physical discipline of boys as a means of instilling obedience and subordination. The patriarch was effective only if he could impose his will upon and secure the unswerving loyalty of his sons, something the father in Jesus' parable failed to accomplish (Luke 15:11-32). Eventually the adolescent son would become a man and spend his life continuing to learn how and trying to prove it (see the Servant Songs in Isaiah, the model of a cultural hero for males to imitate).

Thus, in today's verses the sacred author reflects that Jesus, a very human Mediterranean male, recognized the destiny his Father had designed for him. Jesus prayed for deliverance and was indeed heard (deliverance was his exaltation by the Father). The lectionary translation ignores Jesus' Mediterranean cultural experience described in the preceding paragraph when it says: "even though he was son, he learned obedience from what he suffered." That same Greek particle can and should more plausibly be translated: "Precisely because he was a son [in Mediterranean culture], he learned obedience from what he suffered" as all boys do (or ought to) in this culture.

The verses are appropriate for the lenten season and relate to today's gospel (John 12:20-33) in which Jesus reflects upon his death under the image of a grain of wheat which must die to bear much fruit. These reflections will probably raise more questions for modern believers than they will answer. How can we relate to such barbaric—to our way of understanding—relationships between fathers and sons? If one must die to gain eternal life, why must some suffer so long before death, especially when the condition can be neither eliminated nor alleviated while others are spared this experience? As a cancer patient said to a sociologist in the hospice: "Three hours on the cross is easy. Try a lifetime of cancer."

Palm Sunday
of the Lord's Passion
Philippians 2:6-11

[Contemporary scholarship identifies three distinct letters in Philippians: Letter A = 4:10-20 (in which Paul acknowledges receiving a gift; it is a receipt for aid); Letter B = 1:1–3:1a; 4:4-7, 21-23 (in which Paul having heard of problems in the community exhorts to unity and joy); and Letter C = 3:1b–4:3, 8-9 (in which Paul addresses problems caused by wandering Judaizing missionaries). Scholars who identify three letters, date A and B probably from 54–57 A.D.; Letter C some time later, perhaps 57–58 A.D. All came from Paul imprisoned in Ephesus. Those who identify two letters (combining B and C into one–B), date A to 58–60 A.D. and B to 62 A.D. when Paul was imprisoned in Rome. Year C draws from letters B and C.] Intra-community squabbles about how to live the gospel threatened to divide the Philippians. Paul exhorts them to put aside differences, close ranks, and pursue the virtue of humility after the pattern of Jesus (vv. 1-5). Then, in this well-known hymn (vv. 6-11), Paul presents Jesus as a model for the Philippians to imitate. Scholars agree that this hymn was composed prior to and independently of this letter. It has two sections: vv. 6-8 describes Jesus' humiliation (a shameful thing in this culture); while vv. 9-11 tell how God exalted him to unimaginable honor. Paul uses this hymn to exert moral pressure on the Philippians.

Many commentators see in v. 6 an implicit contrast between Adam who wanted to exploit likeness to God for selfish purposes and Jesus who did not. The verses contain many allusions to Genesis 1–3. In the Israelite tradition, being godlike means being immune from death (Wis 2:23). These verses compare the human Jesus with the human Adam (it is not a reference to pre-existent Jesus who became human). They contrast Jesus' refusal as the final Adam to seek equality with God but highlight his humility and obedience to God in accepting mortality with the first Adam's arrogance and disobedience. He sought to be equal to God as immortal, disobeyed God, and was cursed by God.

By his shameful death, Jesus was humiliated, a major tragedy in this honor-driven culture. But God loved Jesus and exalted him. Thus the basic meaning of Jesus who died and was raised is that he was humiliated and exalted, by God of course. The phrase "on the cross" disturbs the poetry of the hymn and was very likely added by Paul to underscore the degree of Jesus' humiliation. In response (vv. 9-11), God exalted Jesus to rule over the entire universe. Jesus is Lord, the same word used in the Greek Bible to be spoken instead of YHWH. The one who in total obedience took on the low rank of slave now by God's own commission is universal Lord.

To appreciate this hymn, one needs to remember some key elements of honor cultures. First, although one is rightly entitled to ascribed honor (usually by birth), it is also important not to give the impression that one seeks to augment that honor by impinging on others. Thus, all people learn to practice "cultural humility," that is, staying one step behind one's rightful place. Others clearly see that such a person is no threat to their honor. More than this, others will summon this person to his or her rightful, honorable place.

Though this hymn may appear on a surface reading to reflect the reward of cultural humility, in actuality it does not. The hymn rather points to value reversal: shame leads to honor. In other words, Jesus didn't just politely state his humility, confident that someone would raise him to his proper place. He willingly accepted humiliation in the manner of his death. This is something Jesus' culture would not only not have expected but also would not have encouraged. Thus, any culture like that of our ancestors in the faith who live by honor and shame values would be "shocked" by this message of value-reversal: shame will lead to honor. This hymn presents that notion masterfully. It is likely that with this hymn Paul intended to propose an example for the Philippians to imitate given the situation in which they found themselves.

A second consideration is to keep in mind that Philippi was a Roman colony most of whose citizens were retired from the military. They had strong ties to Rome and would be quite willing to participate in the imperial cult, that is, acknowledging Caesar as divine. It is therefore plausible that Paul is vigorously arguing against such participation. His use of certain words (Lord), proposed gestures (bending the knee), mention of an empire (Phil 2:10), and the acclamation "Jesus is Lord" all echo the language of the imperial cult but speak instead of Jesus. Paul is deliberately commanding the Philippians to acknowledge Jesus as Lord rather than Caesar. This, however, is a treasonous act. What course of action would a retired military person who is devoted to Rome but believes in Jesus choose?

Finally, the downward-upward movement of Jesus' life (humiliation/ exaltation; Phil 2:6-8, 9-11) is reflected in Paul's life. He voluntarily abandons all advantages (Phil 3:4-8) in obedience to God. Then, as slave of God (Phil 1:1), Paul carries this obedience (Phil 1:16) to the point that he might—like Jesus—die a shameful death (Phil 1:20) confident that his glory is to come (Phil 3:10-11). The pattern resonates in the lives of Timothy and Epaphroditus as well. The three live in unselfish obedience and service and are a foil to the self-seeking and selfishness that have crept into the Philippian church.

Of course, today's gospel (Mark 14:1–15:47), the Passion of Jesus, presents in significant more detail the shameful end of Jesus' life which God reversed a short while later. It also reflects the choice Jesus made between acknowledging his identity and relationship to God and capitulating to his interrogators. Value reversal is a sobering meditation for people in any culture. So too is loyalty. Holy Week provides yet another opportunity to reflect on the death of Jesus and the challenge it poses to all believers.

Easter Sunday–Easter Vigil
Romans 6:3-11

[See John J. Pilch, *The Triduum and Easter Sunday: Breaking Open the Scriptures* (Collegeville: The Liturgical Press, 2000).]

In Romans 5–8 Paul highlights God's love and exhorts the believers living in Rome to "consider yourselves dead to sin and alive to God in Christ Jesus" (6:11). Sin in the singular is noteworthy. Paul is not talking about some sort of human failing. Rather, his Greek word for sin is more correctly understood as a force or a power that drives a person toward an almost unavoidable proneness to failure or to committing an evil deed. Remember that Mediterranean culture views human beings as subject to nature rather than as controlling nature. Nature, in the Mediterranean world, includes an invisible world of powers and forces which mischievously, capriciously, or sometimes even with deliberate calculation intervene in human life and cause human beings to behave in ways that displease God. This world of power and forces is the context in which Paul understands sin.

The good news in Paul's passage is that Jesus' death and resurrection have destroyed the effectiveness of this force or power called sin. It would be very welcome news to the Mediterranean way of thinking. While some people in this world use amulets, gestures, or incantations to ward off evil, believers through baptism are intimately united with the very one who has defeated the source of all evil.

But people still fail and still commit sins. It is to this situation that Paul speaks when he exhorts his letter recipients thus: thanks to baptism our old self was crucified (v. 6) and we are now "alive to God in Christ Jesus" (v. 11); therefore, we should live accordingly.

Easter Sunday
Colossians 3:1-4 or 1 Corinthians 5:6b-8

Colossians 3:1-4. Written by a creative admirer of Paul perhaps between A.D. 63 and 90, this letter presents Jesus as the cosmic Messiah and explains what it means for Christians to be exclusively devoted to his service. The letter is addressed to believers living in Colossae, a town in southwestern Turkey near Laodicea not far from modern Pammukale. Today's verses begin the paraenetic, that is, hortatory section of the letters. The message is simple. Since believers through baptism have been raised with Jesus, they ought to focus on matters pertaining to alternate reality (what is above) rather than getting bogged down in material reality (the world in which we live). The message of today's first reading and the gospel have some real-life consequences: this selection puts that in focus.

1 Corinthians 5:6b-8. This most appropriate reading for the feast of the Resurrection is drawn from the letter written around 54 A.D. in which Paul deals more extensively with the physical, human body than in any other letter. For the most part, Paul is concerned with orifices. Our ancestors in the faith realized that orifices were weak points on the body through which it could be penetrated and therefore polluted. In 1 Corinthians 5–7 he focuses on the genitals, a major bodily orifice. The fuller context of today's reading (vv. 1-8) is an incestuous marriage or concubinage between a man and his step-mother. Today's verses have been carved away from this larger segment.

Paul draws an analogy between the effect of yeast and the social consequences of this incestuous union ("not found even among pagans!"). The ancients did not fully understand the fermentation process stimulated by yeast in dough and in saccharine liquids, but they knew how to make practical use of yeast in leavening bread and brewing beer. In Paul's view, the incestuous relationship is a pollutant that threatens the social body, that is, the community of believers, and the marriage partner.

In today's verses, Paul presents the rationale for his thinking. Christ the Paschal Lamb has ended the time of leaven, "the old yeast, the yeast of malice and wickedness." Therefore, it is time to get rid of that old yeast as Israelites did at Passover time. Christians are called to be a new lump of dough, yeast-free, "unleavened bread of sincerity and truth." They must strive to maintain the unity of the social body of the Church. This, of course, is the point of the feast we celebrate today, the resurrection of Jesus, which has important behavioral consequences for the community and all its individual members.

Second Sunday of Easter
1 John 5:1-6

[For introductory information to 1 John see the Third Sunday of Easter.] The first four verses of today's reading focus on love, hence continue the author's attack upon the Secessionists. These claim to love, but in the sacred author's view, they lie. His argument is that everyone who believes Jesus is the Messiah is a child of God. Of course, the Secessionists believed this, as did the Johannine community. The author continues: every one who loves the parent loves the child (his argument is generic; there is no reason for translating father with an upper case letter). Conversely, loving the children is a way of loving the parent. So if the Secessionists do not love Johannine believers, they cannot really love God. And if they say that they love members of their group, they are not children of God because their faith is imperfect, hence they have no brothers to love. Further, the Secessionists claim to love God but do not emphasize keeping the commandments. But true love is obedient love, and obedient the Secessionists are not. Lest his own followers get discouraged and submit to pressures from the Secessionists, the author reminds them that commandments (proper behavior) are not burdensome for true children of God.

Johannine scholars acknowledge that vv. 5-9 are very obscure and difficult to interpret. This is a splendid example of high context writing. Surely the letter recipients could read between the lines and supply what the author was presupposing. The Secessionists apparently said that Jesus was the Messiah, the Son of God, who became such when he "came by water," as revealed by the Spirit. The author of 1 John broadens this by alluding to the crucifixion of Jesus and the flow of blood and water from his side (John 19:34). According to the Torah flowing blood was proper so that it could be sprinkled, and the water is not that of baptism (as the Secessionists would claim) but the water then flowed with the blood. The testimony of the beloved disciple to this event continues in the tradition of the Johannine community. The Spirit is still bearing witness.

The significance of witnesses derives from Deut 19:15, which requires two or three. Throughout the gospel of John, multiple witnesses are cited (John 8:18; 5:31-40). This was a technique used by the Johannine community in their arguments with fellow Israelites concerning the divinity of Jesus. Here the author summons it in his debate with the Secessionists over the humanity of Jesus. The Secessionists point to the witness of the Baptist testifying that the incarnation alone is sufficient. The author of 1 John summons three: Spirit, water, blood. How? On a symbolic level, the reference is to sacramental actions familiar to the Johannine Community: Spirit = anointing (see 2 John 2:20, 27); water = baptism (John 3:5); blood = Eucharist (John 6:51-58). Sacraments bear witness to the saving nature of Jesus' death: they constitute people as children of God, nourish them with heavenly food and drink, and they are actions by which true believers share in the action by which Jesus conquered the world (John 16:33).

The pairing of this reading from 1 John with today's gospel (John 20:19-31) is very appropriate. Johannine scholars point out that this section of 1 John seems to have borrowed themes and phrases from the gospel. Jesus gives the Spirit to his disciples. The author's concluding remarks remind his readers that these things were written "that you may come to believe Jesus is Messiah, the Son of God, and through this faith have life in his name." Who doesn't want life in the name of Jesus?

Third Sunday of Easter
1 John 2:1-5a

This is not a letter so much as it is an exhortation to Johannine believers. We do not know the author's identity; he is not the author of the gospel. The document was written after the gospel, perhaps around A.D. 100. His intent is to strengthen the community against those who have broken away (Secessionists) and who misunderstand and misrepresent the true identity and importance of Jesus (4:2-3). They do not show love for fellow believers (2:9-11; 3:10-24; 4:7-21).

The community for which this document was intended represents a third stage of development in the Johannine community. The first phase (pre-gospel, from mid-50s to late-80s) was marked by expulsion from the synagogue (John 9:22; 16:2) and growing animosity between those who accepted Jesus as Messiah and those who didn't. Phase two is the period in which the gospel is being written (ca. A.D. 90). Scars from expulsion are slow to heal because of continuing persecution (John 16:2-3), and antipathy toward "the Judeans" on the part of believers in Jesus grows. In reaction to the rejection of Jesus, the Johannine group develops a "high christology" (eclipsing the humanity of Jesus), which sets the group at odds with other groups that believe in Jesus. Phase three (ca. A.D. 100, the time when the three letters of John were probably written) involves in-group fighting between various Johannine groups who differ in their understanding and interpretation of Jesus. This is the setting for reading and appreciating 1 John.

What position of the Secessionists is being challenged in today's verses? They claimed to be in communion with God despite walking in darkness (1:6ab). They boasted that they were free from sin (1:8a). They denied having sinned (1:9a). Today's verses counter these "boasts" and may represent a primitive stage of the Johannine tradition since they identify Jesus as the "paraclete" (advocate, intercessor, or counselor). In the gospel, the Spirit/Paraclete is "another Paraclete" (John 14:16), suggesting that this was one role or function Jesus fulfilled for the community. Here the exalted Jesus is a paraclete whose function is to intercede on behalf of those who have sinned. More than that, Jesus is expiation for our sins and those of the whole world.

Further, Secessionists claimed to know God but didn't worry about not keeping the commandments. They claimed an intimate knowledge of God while at the same time saw no relationship with or even necessity to live God's way of life proposed in the commandments. Indeed the one commandment they ignore is the command to love one another as Jesus has loved us! This they definitely are not doing. The sacred author calls these people "liars."

In today's gospel (Luke 24:35-48), the risen Jesus opened his disciples' minds to understand the Scriptures. The author of 1 John attempted to do the same for his followers so that they might more vigorously resist the attractive appeals of the Secessionists.

Fourth Sunday of Easter
1 John 3:1-2

Key to understanding these verses is a proper interpretation of the word "world" (Greek: *kosmos*). In the Hellenistic period (300 B.C. to A.D. 300), "world" referred to God's created universe, the earth in contrast to the sky, the inhabited earth, the place of human society, and humanity. Modern understanding and usage of the word are similar. While the Johannine community sometimes used this word to refer to God's creation (John 11:9; 17:5, 24; 21:25), most of the time it refers to humanity, human beings. Specifically, in the Johannine community "world" means Israelites. "Jesus answered him [the high priest]: 'I have spoken publicly to the world. I have always taught in a synagogue or in the temple area where all the Judeans gather, and in secret I have said nothing" (John 18:20). "God so loved the world [that is, the Israelites] that he gave his only Son . . ." (John 3:16). Thus in today's verses, John's faithful community are rightfully called children of God because they accepted Jesus (John 1:10-12), while the Secessionists (the world, or the Israelites who did not accept Jesus) refuse to recognize their fellow Israelites as children of God because the Secessionists refuse to recognize Jesus as Son. (The Greek word *teknon* is a technical Johannine term for describing divine sonship or daughtership; son, *huios,* is reserved for Jesus' relationship to God.)

In the end, the fullness of the believers' identity will be revealed. They will realize that they are like God, for every one will see God clearly. Then their knowledge of God will be similar to what Jesus claims in today's gospel (John 10:11-18): "The Father knows me and I know the Father." The Easter season, which celebrates the resurrection of Jesus and his appearances to his friends, is a tantalizing promise of the experiential knowledge of God all believers look forward to attaining.

Fifth Sunday of Easter
1 John 3:18-24

The polemics of the Secessionists have raised doubts in the community. Their argument is: since believers already possess eternal life through faith in Jesus, behavior has no bearing on salvation. In reply, the sacred author urges that believers must pay more than lip service to love: they must demonstrate its authenticity in deeds. A believer cannot claim to belong to the truth (which is a way of describing what has been revealed in Jesus and appropriated in faith by those who have become children of God) and not love other believers.

Because of the Secessionists, believers were losing self-confidence. What about their sins? Were they really forgiven? Why do their hearts condemn them? The sacred author urges them to remove all doubts. If a believer does what is pleasing to God (keep the commandments, especially to love all believers), God will do what is pleasing to them (their petitions will be answered, requests fulfilled). The Johannine commandment is to believe in Jesus and to love one another (v. 23, in contrast to the synoptic tradition Mark 12:28-31 and parallels). To believe in Jesus is to have faith in God whose Son Jesus is and who has sent Jesus to us. The believers' response is to love all and the result is intimate union with God. This emphasis on Jesus incarnate is yet another counter-offensive to the Secessionists who denied Jesus in the flesh.

In today's gospel (John 15:1-8), Jesus described the intimate union between himself and his followers with the vine imagery. The author of 1 John spells out the behavior required to maintain this union. What else is needed?

Sixth Sunday of Easter
1 John 4:7-10

Once again it is important to keep the Secessionists in mind in order to properly interpret these verses. The Secessionists, who were once Johannine Christians and whose vocabulary also included "love," had a different understanding of what God did in Jesus. It is probably fair to say that they believed God's love for human beings (which existed from eternity) became manifest in the incarnation. The Johannine Christians would insist that the incarnation also includes the life and death of Jesus, something the Secessionists denied. Likely, the Secessionists considered salvation a *fait accompli,* there was nothing more that human beings need do. The Johannine group of believers insisted that behavior was important, notably loving one another. Recall that in the Mediterranean world, love does not involve affection and sentiment as much as it involves group-glue, the determination to keep the community together, whole, and integral.

The familiar and oft-repeated phrase "God is love" in its context here communicates three things: that God has an only beloved Son; that God freely willed to share this Son even to the point of death; that God did this for the forgiveness of our sins that we might have life through Jesus' salvific deed. The gospel for this Sunday (John 15:9-17) resonates very well with this second reading. Love that is willing to die for one's friends has always been admired. To accept that opportunity when it presents itself is a challenge all believers hope they can recognize and accept.

The Ascension of the Lord
Ephesians 1:17-23 or Ephesians 4:1-13

[For brief introduction, see Fifteenth Sunday in Ordinary Time.]

Ephesians 1:17-23. These verses are an intercessory prayer on behalf of the letter recipients. The chief hope of the letter writer is that believers grow in knowledge of God, God's activity, and God's gifts. God raised Jesus from the dead and gave him a place of honor next to God in the sky. This makes Jesus a co-regent or ruler with God. In Jesus' risen position he is exalted over angelic and cosmic forces which have such serious impact on the lives of ordinary human beings. Principalities, authorities, powers, and dominions are celestial personages, astral beings who are now subject to Christ. Further, Jesus is head over the Church which is his body. In this letter, however, Paul's basic idea is further developed by the one who wrote in his name. Now the Church, Christ's body, benefits from God's all-embracing plan, and one of the benefits is to share in the dominion which the head, Jesus, has.

Ephesians 4:1-13. [For commentary on Eph 4:1-6, see Seventeenth Sunday in Ordinary Time.] After reflecting upon the unity of the Church in vv. 3-6, the sacred author considers the diversity of Church offices within this body in vv. 7-13. He cites Ps 68:19 in a form that does not reflect either the Hebrew or the Greek version. The biblical text says, "you

[Lord God] received men as gifts," while the citation in Eph 4:8 says "he [Jesus] gave gifts to men." Scholars believe that the sacred author is quoting from a collection of testimonies *(testimonia)* which were gathered together to help preachers as they presented the community's ongoing and developing understanding of Jesus raised and ascended. Certain passages of the Old Testament quite in contrast to their original meaning were interpreted as "testimonies" to gospel facts, or as somehow reflecting the intention of God which was fulfilled in those facts. Psalm 68 is considered a testimony to the ascension of Jesus. Clearly biblical texts are rearranged and recast in such a way as to present new information and thereby serve to construct theology for the Messianist community. The idea in Ephesians is that Jesus risen and now ascended is the one who bestows gifts upon the Church.

The "gifts" of Ps 68:19 are interpreted here as offices within the Church. Apostles and prophets belong to the period of foundation of the Church (see Eph 2:20), that is, they belong to a period now past. These were succeeded by evangelists, shepherds, and teachers which are ministries prominent in the Church of the letter-writer (after Paul's death). Their task is to guide the holy ones toward stronger unity of belief, deeper knowledge of Jesus, and maturity measuring up to "the full stature of Christ."

Today's gospel (Mark 16:15-20) is drawn from the "longer ending" of Mark which is likely based on Luke 24:50-51 and Acts 1:9-11. It reports the event of the ascension of Jesus, while the import of this event for the believing community is spelled out in Ephesians. All the readings offer an opportunity for modern believers to learn and appreciate how our ancestors in the faith used their scriptural traditions to resolve questions about their beliefs. While modern approaches to interpreting the Bible do not follow this path any longer, they would benefit from learning how the ancients used insights thus gained to strengthen their faith.

Seventh Sunday of Easter
1 John 4:11-16

"No one has ever seen God" (v. 12) was something upon which the Johannine community and the Secessionists would agree. This was likely a maxim from the struggles both groups had in the synagogue before expulsion around the year A.D. 90. The gospel claimed that the exalted Jesus was the only one who had seen God, while Judeans in general made this claim for Moses and Elijah. From this maxim, the author of 1 John moves ahead to focus upon God dwelling in us (something already mentioned in v. 10). This is a far greater intimacy than seeing God, and it is manifest when believers love one another. The proof of this indwelling is the Spirit, the giver of life (John 6:63), the one who has begotten the community as God's children. Because of this, they have a special privilege: they have seen not God as God is, but God in Jesus, the Father in the Son. Secessionists agreed that the Son of God was indeed sent by God, but they would not agree that "sent" included the notion of ministry and salvific death as the Johannine community does. The concluding v. 16, "God is love," seems to echo v. 8. Yet while in the former the stress is on the sending of the Son, the latter by its context emphasizes God dwelling in the believer who abides in love.

These reflections match well with today's gospel (John 17:11b-19) in which Jesus prays that his disciples "may be one just as we are one." It may be difficult in our individualistic culture to appreciate the high value placed upon unity and integrity of a community in collectivistic societies. That is what these readings reflect, and maintaining the integrity of the community that remained after the departure of the Secessionists was the author's main objective. To what extent would we go to maintain the unity of our communities?

The Vigil of Pentecost
Romans 8:22-27

According to Paul, three things persuade us of the greatness of the glory or intimate share in God's life which is the destiny of each believer: the testimony of creation (vv. 19-22), the conviction of believers (vv. 23-25), and the testimony of the Spirit (vv. 26-30). Because of Adam's sin (Gen 3:15-17), material nature was cursed, subject to decay itself just like the human beings for whom it had been created. This solidarity in punishment also entails solidarity in redemption. So creation eagerly awaits and groans in labor pains until that final state of glory will be definitively restored. This reflection has special cultural significance. In general, Mediterranean cultures of antiquity recognized that they had absolutely no control over material creation. They were subject to it; they had to suffer and endure it. Thus our ancestors in the faith believed that because of Adam's sin, human beings had no control over nature, yet the redemption of Adam would include the redemption of material creation as well.

What is the basis for Paul's confidence? He draws insight from the notion of first fruits of a harvest (vv. 23-25). When offered to God, these first fruits consecrated the entire harvest and became, as it were, down-payment, pledge, or guarantee of what was still to come. The Spirit serves this purpose for believers (vv. 26-30). Since the believer is already son/child of God (Rom 8:15), the full implementation of this will include the redemption of the body.

In saying that "we do not know how to pray as we ought" (v. 26), Paul seems to contradict what he said just a few verses earlier, that the Spirit prompts us to pray with confidence: "Abba, my Father" (Rom 8:15). It is possible that Paul offers a corrective here to enthusiasm, namely, an exaggerated emphasis on the gifts of the Spirit. It is always possible to be overconfident. The truth is, of course, that because of natural human shortcomings, the Spirit adds its intercessions to our inadequate expressions. God knows this. In today's gospel (John 7:37-39), John illuminates Jesus' statement as a reference to the Spirit which believers would receive. Paul in his turn explains what that Spirit does for believers.

Pentecost
1 Corinthians 12:3b-7, 12-13 or
Galatians 5:16-25

1 Corinthians 12:3b-7, 12-13. [For brief background, see Second Sunday in Ordinary Time.] Even a cursory reading of these verses indicates that Paul is insisting on unity. The Corinthian community was so torn by competing party loyalties and dissension that Paul repeatedly exhorts to unity at every opportunity in this letter. The "spirit-people" in Corinth were viewed as the cause of disunity, in part because they were vaunting the Spirit, themselves, and their gifts from the Spirit above others who did not possess such gifts.

It is very difficult for Western individualists to appreciate the harm done by competition in a culture whose core value is honor. By birth, all people in such a culture have ascribed honor. It is shameful and wrong to attempt to improve that status. The cultural obligation is to maintain and preserve it. Cooperation, harmony, and unity are the preferred and honorable values in a collectivistic society.

The combination of select verses for today's reading highlight two powerful arguments that Paul mounts against such divisive competition. One argument is based on how three heavenly figures relate to each other. After admitting that the Spirit does indeed grant various gifts, forms of service, and workings, Paul notes—in an apparent hierarchic ordering—that the Spirit, the Lord, and God live in harmony and not in rivalry or competition. God, of course, is sovereign and holds the highest place on the honor map (see 1 Cor 11:3;

15:27-28). And the authentic spirit acknowledges that Jesus has a special position: "Jesus is Lord." Thus, after God, Jesus enjoys the next maximum status, and the Spirit holds third place as servant of the Lord Jesus. The three are not equal in role or status, yet they live harmoniously in heaven. The Spirit and the Spirit's gifts, therefore, should not disrupt the order God has willed for the world. The second argument is based on the human body which consists of different parts, all of which must work together harmoniously lest damage occur to the body.

This exaggerated sense of self-esteem and exalted status among the "spirit people" amounts to a denial of authority. Their understanding of the freedom bestowed upon them by the Spirit calls into question God's will for specific patterns of roles, statuses, and orderly relationships on earth and in heaven. Paul argues that the pattern existing in heaven ought to be mirrored on earth. In the concluding verses (12-13), Paul declares that not only is the diversity of gifts among human beings unified in the same Spirit, but the diversity of ethnic groups (Israelites and non-Israelites) and roles (slaves or free persons) is similarly unified in the "one" Spirit.

Galatians 5:16-25. Finally, Paul draws practical conclusions from the preceding four chapters of his letter. He urges those who have slipped in their resolve or who have backslided in their status to dig in, to stand firm, to yield not another inch to anyone. At issue is a return to circumcision which Paul opposed and rejected as a requirement for non-Israelites to become followers of Jesus.

Once again tugging at the letter recipients' emotions ("brothers and sisters," v. 13), Paul presents another understanding of "freedom." He discourages using freedom for unfettered self-indulgence. "Serve one another through love" (v. 13). Literally, the Greek verb translated here as "serve one another" should be rendered "render slave service" to one another. The Israelite understanding which Paul reflects is that no human person is ever absolutely free, subject to no one. The Exodus freed the Israelites from Egyptian bondage so that they might serve (render slave service to) God more faithfully. By raising Jesus from the dead, God gave an opportunity for those who believe in Jesus to attain a new freedom, a freedom for a new kind of slave service. For those united in Jesus, secondary differences are not important (gender, social status, ethnicity). What really counts is "faith working through love" (Gal 5:6).

To make his instruction concrete, Paul draws on two favorite images: flesh and spirit. Flesh refers to the human person as entirely self-reliant, weak, earthbound, unredeemed. Spirit refers to the knowing and willing core of the individual, that part of a human person most suitable for receiving and responding to God's Spirit. Paul's advice: Live by the Spirit! Walk according to the prompting of the Spirit! What does this mean in the concrete? With regard to how believers should behave toward one another, Paul lists actions to be avoided (5:19-21) and actions to be performed (5:22-23). The deeds to be avoided reflect a way of life rooted in the flesh. They can be clustered into four groups: sexual aberrations (the first three items), heathen worship (the next two), social evils (seven items, many in the plural suggesting numerous and repeated occurrences), and intemperance (the last three). All of them are failures against justice and love, hardly a fitting lifestyle for those who accept the rule of God in their lives.

The main deed to be performed is love, along with nine other representative desirable qualities that should characterize a believer's relationships with other believers (5:22-23). The final verses sum up Paul's feelings. Those who have accepted Jesus have definitively, once and for always put aside the way of the flesh and should live, walk, and be led by the spirit.

The gospel (John 20:19-23 or John 15:26-27; 16:12-15) describes yet other gifts of the Spirit (power to forgive and retain sins; guidance to all truth) intended to maintain unity in the community.

Trinity Sunday
Romans 8:14-17

A very important result of being led (or perhaps better, shaped) by the Spirit is that one becomes a true child of God. Though this is the first time this concept appears in this letter, it would not catch Paul's audience by surprise. It was a widely accepted notion in the ancient world even outside Judaism. In his speech to the Athenians (Acts 17:28), Paul quotes Aratus of Soli, a third-century B.C. poet from Cilicia: "For we too are his offspring." In Judaism, Israel was understood as God's child or son (Exod 4:22-23; Isa 1:2-4; Hos 1:10; etc). The Spirit or force we have received, however, is not one that would cast us back into fear, even a reverential fear. Rather, this Spirit says we are dear to God, we are God's very own adopted children.

While adoption was a wide-spread legal practice in the Greco-Roman world, it was not a common practice in Israel. Some scholars would say this option didn't exist. For this reason, Paul is quite likely not drawing on this legal practice which would be mystifying to his letter recipients. It is more plausible that he is drawing on the notion that grew and developed out of Hos 1:10 (Heb 2:1): once God said to them "you are not my people," but later it will be said to them: you are "sons of the living God." Earlier in this letter, Paul lists adoption as one of Israel's privileges (Rom 9:4).

Whatever the case, the idea is startling. Kinship was the focal social institution of the ancient Mediterranean world.

Kin marked one's primary in-group. All others are the out-group. Thus to become part of God's very own in-group is quite amazing. Further, not only does the Spirit make this kinship relationship with God possible, the same Spirit gives the ability to recognize and be aware of it. Such people can say with confidence and conviction: "Abba, Father." Though suffering and tribulation might shake this confidence, the Spirit strengthens that conviction.

The good news gets even better, for children can also inherit. Earlier (Rom 4:13ff.) Paul noted that Abraham "would inherit the world" because he became right with God on the basis of faith rather than "through [works of] the law." In this way even non-Israelites can share in that inheritance, as joint heirs with the Messiah, the primary heir (see Rom 8:29). Inheritance, however, entails an obligation to share in death and resurrection of Jesus too, for these were an integral part of his life. Paul uses two compound verbs in Greek that believers must suffer with the Messiah in order to be glorified with him.

The gospel (Matt 28:16-20) offers an interesting contrast. Some scholars point out that since Jesus' concern through the gospel is with "the lost sheep of the House of Israel" and shows no interest in the Gentile world ("go nowhere among the Gentiles," Matt 10:5), this final injunction should probably be interpreted in this way: "Go therefore and make disciples of [all the members of the house of Israel scattered in] all nations." If this is acceptable, then Paul and his generation of believers took a significant step forward by including Gentiles. What steps forward can modern believers take?

Eleventh Sunday in Ordinary Time
2 Corinthians 5:6-10

The main point Paul makes is that he aspires to please God and God alone (v. 9) so that he might receive his proper recompense (v. 10). What prompts this declaration? His opponents in Corinth concluded that Paul's sufferings and tribulations weakened his claim to be an apostle. Why would God treat an apostle this way, and what good is a sickly and weak apostle? Paul argues that suffering and tribulation are integral to a believer's life. He insists that he remains courageous in the face of danger or testing.

One of the difficulties in reading English translations of Paul's letters is recognizing when he is "quoting" his opponents and when he is presenting his response. The Corinthians considered human bodily existence as an obstacle to union with Jesus: "While we are here in the body, we are away from the Lord" (v. 6). Paul replies: "I would rather leave the body and be with the Lord" (v. 7). The opponents set up a contrast between "here" and "there." Paul replies that he moves progressively through life from "here" to "there" with the Lord. So whether one is away from the Lord (at home, in the body) or with the Lord (after death) is of less consequence than striving to please him.

Finally, Paul draws on another familiar theme: judgment and receiving recompense according to what one has done

(v. 10). Of special note is the importance of the body's activities in the final judgment. Unlike his opponents, Paul holds the body in high esteem (though he frequently complains of being frail and likely to die).

Just as Jesus taught in parables (Mark 4:26-34) whose meanings were not immediately self-evident, so did Paul use rhetoric and a style in his letters which pose a challenge to modern readers. Cross-cultural communication isn't easy, but efforts to understand it pay rich dividends.

Twelfth Sunday in Ordinary Time
2 Corinthians 5:14-17

Our ancestors in the faith, and notably Paul, divided time in terms of "time before Jesus" and "time after Jesus." Similar divisions included: then vs. now (Gal 4:8-9); once but now (Gal 4:3-7); mystery hidden vs. mystery now revealed (1 Cor 2:6-10); and mystery promised vs. mystery now given (Titus 1:2ff.). The time after Jesus is qualitatively different from the time before Jesus. The new context is one of holiness and sinlessness as the normative way of life for all believers.

In this new state, the love shown by Jesus who selflessly died for all becomes a new model of authentic human existence. The pattern of Jesus' death becomes the pattern according to which those who benefitted must now live. The new life Jesus has gained for all must be made manifest in a concern for others.

Old ways of judgment (according to the flesh, that is, the criteria of the unredeemed world) must be replaced. Paul admits that as a Pharisee, he misjudged Jesus because he used the wrong criteria. Now, however, Paul knows Jesus differently, he views Jesus from a different perspective. The concluding exhortation is that whoever belongs to the community of believers (whoever is in Christ) is a new creation. Therefore, within such a context, the standard of judgment must change, too.

Mark (4:35-41) in today's gospel recounts an occasion on which the disciples saw Jesus in a fresh light when he stilled the storm. Understanding Jesus isn't as easy as some might think. The disciples and Paul had to work toward a correct understanding. Why would modern believers think they have an advantage over Paul and the disciples?

Thirteenth Sunday in Ordinary Time
2 Corinthians 8:7, 9, 13-15

The architects of the lectionary have strung select verses together to reshape Paul's original thought (see Sloyan). It is important to recognize this because this second letter to the Corinthians is composed of at least two letters (some would say as many as five), and chapters 8–9 occasion discussion as to whether they should be attached to chapters 1–7 or considered yet another letter. In these reflections, we follow the opinion that they continue from chapter 7. Those who would undertake a longer and more detailed study of Paul's Corinthian correspondence can find and evaluate the details of the argumentation (Murphy-O'Connor 1997).

In today's select verses, Paul is urging the Corinthians to be generous in a collection being taken up for the needs of the Jerusalem church. Ordinarily in this culture, people relate to each other by means of an implicit dyadic contract (I do you a favor, you owe me; you pay back my favor, I owe you; etc.). This is also called balanced reciprocity. It would seem that this is the principle Paul is invoking here. He prefaced his request by flattering the Corinthians with regard to their spiritual gifts, the very things in which they took excessive pride and which occasioned Paul's corrective to them about these things in 1 Corinthians. Next, he presents the image of Jesus who by despoiling himself made others rich.

Finally, he lays out his request: from your surplus send what you can (without despoiling yourself) to help the church in Jerusalem. If you should ever become needy, they will be able and willing to help you in return. To bolster his request, Paul cites Exod 16:18 concerning the manna: "he that gathered much had nothing over; he that gathered little, had no lack." Everyone had enough, neither too little nor surplus.

In today's gospel (Mark 5:21-43) Jesus performs two life-renewing deeds: he heals the woman with the menstrual irregularity and raises Jairus' daughter from the dead. Few have shared in Jesus' life-giving abilities, but all believers are capable of the life-restoring strategy Paul proposes to the Corinthians: from your surplus help those in need that they may have a meaningful life. What kind of life-giving and meaning-restoring activities are open to modern believers?

Fourteenth Sunday in Ordinary Time
2 Corinthians 12:7-10

These verses belong to letter B (2 Cor 10:1–13:13), a contrast to letter A. While tact and control characterized letter A, letter B is filled with unrestrained outrage in which Paul justifies himself but also heaps scorn on his opponents. This, of course, is perfectly normal in the Mediterranean world. Insult is appropriate, and a master of insult is viewed as an honorable person. Paul's Corinthian opponents boasted of visions and revelations which they felt gave them an edge of superiority, even relative to Paul. His counter argument is to demonstrate that he is equal if not superior to these opponents. His superiority is evident not only in his endurance of labors, hardships, dangers, and the like, but most especially in that God's power compensates for his weakness. God said: "My grace is sufficient for you, for power is made perfect in weakness." Indeed, in weakness Paul is strong, and through weakness he is made perfect because God's activity is all the more evident. Lest his enemies remain ignorant, Paul reminds them that he too has had an "abundance of revelations."

The "thorn in the flesh" might have been an illness, a common opinion, but perhaps it is more likely to view this as enemies, people within believing communities who oppose him and direct hostility to him (compare Num 33:55). Jesus encountered similar resistance and hostility in his own home town (Mark 6:1-6). What kind of image do modern believers present to others? Are they perceived as overflowing with divine favor or do they appear weak, buffeted by insults, persecutions, constraints, and the like? How do others respond to this perception?

Fifteenth Sunday in Ordinary Time
Ephesians 1:3-14

These verses from a letter in the Pauline tradition (written probably between A.D. 80–100) are part of the customary blessing (vv. 3-14) with which most of the letters begin. Why should we bless God? Primarily because God chose us in Jesus just as he chose special people before us (see Deut 14:2). Given the gratuitous nature of the choice, one can only marvel and be grateful. Of course, that election involves an obligation: God's chosen people must be holy and without blemish in God's presence. Yet another reason for requiring such holiness and purity is the Ephesian congregation's conviction that it too, perhaps like the Colossians, was convinced that angels were in the midst of the worshiping community (see Eph 3:10; also 2:6). This is similar to the sentiments at Qumran where anyone physically blemished "shall not enter to take their place among the congregation of famous men, for the angels of holiness are among their congregation" (1QSa 2:8-9).

Being chosen is only the first in a series of reasons for blessing God who has also adopted us. Scholars observe that in this culture where family (kinship) is one of the dominant social institutions and is rather extensive and complex, there was no mechanism for adoption. That Paul would reach this conclusion would be an interesting breakthrough. Those who heard this from Paul and his circle would be awed and perhaps even skeptical. God's election bestows incredible honor and far-reaching consequences. The clusters of words and ideas that include beloved, adopted children, redemption, forgiveness of transgression, and sealed with the Spirit reflect early baptismal traditions. Some scholars think this letter was intended for newly baptized believers to help them appreciate the implications of their baptism.

All of this, of course, is God's will, expressed in these verses with the word "mystery." God controls everything: the human world, the angelic, and the cosmic. The mysteries have been revealed to select interpreters, in this instance, Paul who uses this word to summarize the content of the gospel he preaches. Today's gospel (Mark 6:7-13) tells how Jesus summoned twelve and sent them out to preach repentance, cast out demons, and anoint and heal the sick. How reassuring when preachers can share such good news with their listeners.

Sixteenth Sunday in Ordinary Time
Ephesians 2:13-18

In this second of seven sequential readings in Cycle B from an encyclical letter written to many churches in Asia (modern Turkey), a disciple of Paul paints a fascinating picture of an undivided Church even as his vocabulary still reflects a "we" (Israelites) and "you" (non- Israelites) perspective. The actual phrases, those "who once were far off" and those "who were near," reflect spatial imagery. The most visible dividing wall between these two groups surely was the Temple, which featured a "courtyard for non-Israelites" and an inner sanctum reserved for Israelites alone. The message over the entrance to the inner courts reminded non-Israelites: "No person of another nation is to enter . . . and whoever is caught will be personally responsible for that death which ensues."

But the word "enmity" that describes the "dividing wall" suggests that the author is thinking of interpersonal contexts, in-group and out-group hostilities, as is reflected in Peter's realization that such should end (Acts 10:28). The reason given here is that through his death, Jesus has united Israelites and non-Israelites in his body, the Church, as one new humanity. The result is peace between both groups and union with God, just as for individuals the result was reconciliation and peace with God. The hungry disciples and crowds in today's gospel (Mark 6:30-34) stir Jesus to pity and prompt him to teach them many things. Paul's disciple in today's epistle teaches his communities many things about the love and mercy of God. One doesn't need specialized certification to share this good news.

Seventeenth Sunday in Ordinary Time
Ephesians 4:1-6

As customary in this part of the letter, the author begins to exhort the letter recipients to proper conduct. The basis for such conduct has already been presented. All things have been united in Jesus and subjected to him (1:10, 22-23). A new humanity has been created through Jesus' sacrifice (2:15-16). Israelites and non-Israelites alike constitute a united community, the Church (3:4-6). Now it is time to urge that that unity be maintained.

Recalling that Mediterranean culture in general is agonistic helps to appreciate this exhortation to unity. Accepting Jesus as Messiah does not automatically guarantee unanimity in belief and uniformity in practice. We are quite familiar with disagreements among the apostles and disciples regarding requirements for accepting non-Israelites into the community of believers. Even within congregations, such as Corinth, people disagreed depending on which apostle won their allegiance. In this letter, Paul's disciple singles out the virtues of humility, gentleness, patience, and bearing with one another through love. Humility means never giving the slightest indication that one is impinging on the honor of another. Hence one does not insist on rights or honor claims, but stands one step behind one's rightful and deserved place or honor.

Gentleness is the virtue by which a Middle-Easterner would strive to refrain from engaging too vigorously in the daily competition for honor known as challenge and riposte. Patience means making even greater attempts to control the cultural tendency to spontaneous, unreflexive, emotionally driven responses to provocative situations. Such responses can escalate to hostility, erupt in bloodshed, and result in long-standing blood feuds. The key is "bearing with one another through love." Love here is not an affection or emotion; it is group glue. Love in this culture is the commitment to keep a group together, preserve it's unity, and do all to avoid tearing it apart.

Then follows a list of seven areas in which unity should be pursued and displayed: one body, the community; one Spirit, the Spirit that unites rather than divides. All have the same confidence (hope) because of God's call. All recognize one Lord, Jesus to whom everything has been subjected. One faith is very plausibly unity in belief, in accepting the authoritative apostolic tradition (Eph 2:20) and distinguishing it from false teaching (Eph 4:14). This unity makes sense because all have been baptized with one baptism that formally initiates newcomers into one body, a unified community.

Today's gospel (John 6:1-15) is quite clearly about the Eucharist which is not mentioned at all in the epistle. On the other hand, scholars suggest that these verses in Ephesians reflect baptismal ritual in which the "one" phrases may have been liturgical "shouts" which occurred during the sacramental ritual. Modern believers who experience both sacraments have plenty to consider in the reflections by the evangelist and today's letter writer.

Eighteenth Sunday in Ordinary Time
Ephesians 4:17, 20-24

Continuing the hortatory portion of this epistle, the letter writer contrasts the ungodly lifestyle of non-Israelites with the kind of life that new members of the body of Christ should lead. This is traditional opinion presented in stereotypical language and in no way suggests that the letter recipients were guilty of these behaviors. Similar charges against non-Israelites can be found in Rom 1:21-25 echoing Wis 13:1-41. These bad behaviors are all rooted in idolatry, that is, the fact these people did not know the true God. Everyone knew that there were models of virtue among non-Israelites, but when a speaker needed a straw person with immoral behaviors to attack, this stereotypical view of non-Israelite behavior was trotted out. The author of Wisdom presents one of these stock "vice-lists" when he writes: "All is confusion—blood and murder, theft and guile, corruption, faithlessness, turmoil, perjury, disturbance of good men, neglect of gratitude, besmirching of souls, unnatural lust, disorder in marriage, adultery and shamelessness" (Wis 14:25-26).

The distinctive idea of this sacred author is that believers through baptism have put on a new nature (v. 24) and therefore should behave as befits this new nature, namely, in righteousness and holiness of truth. Righteousness is a person's rightful claim to innocence, or a rightful judgment that

91

this is indeed the case. This condition not only sets the believer right with God because God had so willed and effected it, but this is also how the believers ought to treat others. These verses are probably a summary of baptismal instruction emphasizing the need for ongoing conversion ("be renewed in the spirit of your minds"). Anyone who thinks that a once-and-for-all-time event works wonders is deceived. In a sense, Jesus gives this advice to those whom he fed (John 6:24-35). You ate and were satisfied at this time. "Strive after [the tense of the Greek verb designates an ongoing activity] the food that endures for eternal life." Everything worthwhile requires enduring effort.

Nineteenth Sunday in Ordinary Time
Ephesians 4:30–5:2

To properly understand the point of these exhortations, modern Western readers need to recall that the letter recipients—like 80 percent of the people on the face of the planet today—are collectivistic personalities. For such people, the community is paramount; individual identity and purpose derive from membership in the community. For such personalities, the individual is subservient and subordinate to—yes, even expendable for—the group. With this understanding, three things take on greater clarity in today's reading.

First, the author repeats (in Eph 2:20-22) what Paul himself taught quite explicitly: "your [plural] body [singular] is a temple of the Holy Spirit within you [plural], which you [plural] have from God" (1 Cor 6:19). The plurals indicate Paul's belief that the corporate body, the Church, is the temple of the Spirit. Difficulty of perceiving these plural in English translation leave this passage susceptible to misunderstanding and misinterpretation. In the world of our ancestors in the faith, the spirit is never private property, a personal possession. The spirit belongs to the group, informs the group, makes the group its temple.

Thus, the author of Ephesians exhorts, "Do not grieve the Holy Spirit of God," and then proceeds to list behaviors which are divisive in a community. All of these behaviors are threats to the honor and reputation of others. They are shameful behaviors which very clearly destroy the harmonious unity of a group.

Second, the proper behaviors proposed by the author are summed up in the exhortation "walk in love." In collectivistic societies which are typically non-introspective and not psychologically driven, love has little to do with feelings of affection, sentiments of fondness, and warm, glowing affinity. Love in this context is "the value of group attachment and group bonding." Love is the willingness to sacrifice whatever is required in order to maintain group integrity. Forgiveness, or perhaps better the forgoing of retaliation or revenge for besmirched honor, will guarantee "love," that is, it will maintain the unity of the group (see Pilch 1999: 59–64). No one can argue with the motive: "forgive one another, as God in Christ forgave you."

Jesus' fellow ethnics in today's gospel (John 6:41-51) who murmur about his claim to have come down from heaven are only acting out the scenario presumed by the author of Ephesians. Anyone who raises himself above his birth status as Jesus seems to be doing is a threat to the community. Sometimes the evangelist's ideology blunts for the modern reader the shock that Jesus' Middle Eastern peers surely felt. Believers are left to decide which is the preferable course of action: challenge the community values as Jesus does, or strive to preserve the community intact as the author of Ephesians counsels. Perhaps there is a right time for each action.

Twentieth Sunday in Ordinary Time
Ephesians 5:15-20

In these hortatory segments of his letter, the sacred author borrows generously from the Hebrew Scriptures and from catechetical instructions, but he tends to follow a pattern. He uses second person plural forms. He is, after all, addressing collectivistic personalities who typically respect group norms. Second, he coordinates negative and positive advice. Don't continue in ignorance, but understand the will of the Lord. Don't get drunk on wine, but fill up with the Spirit; etc. Third, he includes reasons for his instructions, e.g., debauchery springs from inebriation.

The letter recipients are advised to walk (= live) like wise persons rather than foolish. This is the overarching motif which also appears in the Qumran literature. "Until now the spirits of truth and of injustice feud in the heart of man and they walk in wisdom or folly" (1QS 4:23-24). This is an allusion to the notion that when God created the first earthling, God implanted two drives or inclinations within him (Gen 2:7): one toward good and one toward evil. As the story unfolded, God noticed that the inclination toward evil seemed to prevail (Gen 6:5; 8:21). Instead of behaving wisely, humankind elected to behave foolishly.

The concluding verses invite some reflections about music in the worshiping community. Some scholars have conjectured that singing (psalms, hymns, spiritual songs, etc.) was one way in which the community received prophecy. The plausibility of this conjecture is enhanced when one understands that Middle Eastern music, in general, is based on melodicles, brief (perhaps two or four measure) melodies which when repeated with variations can be hypnotic (see Pilch 1999: 111–6). In other words, this form of music can easily induce altered states of consciousness through which one enters alternate reality and can engage the entire spirit world. The visionary communicates with God, the spirit world, and fellow human beings through music. The exhilarating experience results in attitudes of thanksgiving always and everywhere for everything.

In today's gospel (John 6:51-58), Jesus offers his audience yet another means of intimate communion with himself and the Father: the bread that came down from heaven which he shares with them. The author of Ephesians promotes both a lifestyle and a strategy for achieving such intimacy with the Spirit of God and Jesus. Polls regularly indicate that Americans believe they have had intimate experiences of God and yearn either to have them or continue to have them. A return to the sources and an informed reading of these documents could offer a key.

Twenty-First Sunday in Ordinary Time
Ephesians 5:21-32

These verses belong to the literary form known as "household codes." Though very common in Greco-Roman popular philosophy, they are found in the New Testament only in the Deutero-Paulines (see introduction) and in 1 Peter. In general the codes treat of various relationships: husbands and wives, children and parents, and slaves and masters. Those relationships which in general are of subordinates to superiors cover all the occupants of the household in antiquity.

To properly interpret this household code, it is important to review some basic cultural ideas. These are collectivistic personalities embedded in kinship or surrogate kinship groups. As in all cultures so too in this one persons are socialized into values and duties. We call this social formation or education. Since "household codes" concern kinship, the primary issues will stem from gender and generation, namely, the social expectations of gender identity in a particular family or clan.

It is also important to remember that human rights which emerged in Western history only during the Enlightenment were of no interest in antiquity. The majority of persons in ancient Mediterranean collectivist cultures did not have any rights in the modern legal sense. But they did have duties, and these duties or obligations are what the household codes prescribed not in the sense of new ideas but rather as reminders of how men and women had been socialized. In general, this passage in 'Ephesians reflects the cultural conviction that a husband must treat his wife with respect owed blood relatives, even though she may not be his kin. She in turn must show loyalty to the male in whom she is now embedded, transferring to him the loyalty formerly owed her father.

This passage expands Col 3:18–4:1 by adding reflections on the relationship of Jesus and the Church. Notice two things in this passage: there is a balance of imagery and an exhortation to mutuality. Masculine imagery is reflected in Christ and husband; feminine imagery is clear in Church and wife. The culturally determined division of labor according to gender underpins this balanced imagery. Yet the passage is not presenting ideal marriage relationships for all times and places. Rather, it is discussing the Church and its relationship to Christ. The note of mutuality is sounded in v. 21 (be subordinate to one another). Then Jesus' lordship over the body serves as the model for the husband as head of the wife. Further, the rather uncustomary listing of the husband's obligations presented in vv. 25-33 is associated with Jesus' love for the Church which is his bride. Thus Jesus is the bridegroom who purifies his bride, the Church, in the waters of baptism in order that she might be clothed in holiness and purity.

The concluding verse is very significant. The sacred author clearly states: "this is a great mystery." The reference is to Gen 2:23 whose real meaning was not in the original context but rather in the present, namely, the union of Jesus and the Church. It is this relationship cast into a household code that now becomes the model of union in one flesh between husbands and wives. In the gospel which concludes the "eucharistic discourse" in John (6:60-69), the disciples observe: "This is a hard saying; who can accept it?" It is plausible that the opinion of the sacred author of Ephesians about marriage met with a similar response. Modern believers might respond in like manner to many of the convictions of our ancestors in the faith. Yet surely all would conclude as did the Twelve: "to whom [else] shall we go? You have the words of eternal life."

Twenty-Second Sunday in Ordinary Time
James 1:17-18, 21b-22, 27

This letter was written by an unknown Christian teacher in the name of James of Jerusalem, "brother of the Lord" (Gal 1:19; Matt 13:55; Mark 6:3), probably in the early or middle 60s. The theme of the letter is announced in 1:2-12: the completeness and wholeness of the recipients, of their community, and of their relationship to God (vv. 2-4, revised NAB: "perfect and complete"). Completeness and wholeness are contrasted with incompleteness, fragmentation, and division in vv. 5-9, signaling seven sets of similar contrasts that will follow in the body of the letter, the negative aspect first, then the positive. [For additional background see Third Sunday of Advent, Cycle A.]

Today's verses are part of the first contrast (1:13-17). Negative: no one should deceive self by attributing trials to God, but rather should acknowledge that they stem from human desire (vv. 13-16). Positive: from God, rather, come complete gifts, in response to which believers ought to integrate hearing and doing in their worship. The complete, integral, whole human person lives with all three symbolic body zones perfectly aligned and operating in harmony. The word has been planted in believers (in the heart/eyes zone), hence they should be doers (hands/feet) and not just hearers (mouth/ears zone) of the word. Deluding oneself (v. 22) is equivalent to deluding one's heart (v. 26). The relationship with today's gospel (Mark 7:1-8, 14-15, 21-23) is obvious: the Pharisees say the right things (mouth/ears = honor with lips), but their hearts are far from me (heart/eyes). Jesus points out that their zones are misaligned and operate dysfunctionally. The pseudonymous author of this letter, James the brother of the Lord, takes a similar view of human beings.

What does this have to do with holiness? Believers are to "put away all filthiness and rank growth of wickedness" (v. 21), and instead practice "pure and undefiled" worship before God. Concretely, this means to care for the most vulnerable in the community (orphans and widows, both experiencing a temporary dislocation from ascribed or acquired status) and to remain "unstained" by "the world." In other words, "the world" refers to a polluting society with standards of valuation that differ markedly from those of God's holy people. God's people must resist following the ways of the world but seek rather to be perfect like God is perfect. God cares for the widows and orphans (Ps 67:6), so must those who claim to worship the deity.

Twenty-Third Sunday in Ordinary Time
James 2:1-5

The recipients of this letter are a mix of Israelite and non-Israelite believers in Jesus who live in the dispersion. They are linked with the identity, history, and traditions of the twelve tribes of Israel (1:1). In reality they are a culturally mixed audience from various social strata. There are rich and poor (2:1-13), teachers (3:1-18), and elders (5:14) on one side, and ordinary members on the other. Such a mix brings in its wake a plurality of perspectives and norms concerning appropriate social behavior, tension and conflict between the haves and have-nots, trials, dispiriting strife and divisions within the community, and serious questions about how to relate with non-believing outsiders.

Today's verses indicate that this cultural pluralism and social-economic disequilibrium fomented discrimination between social classes, and the seeking of favor from wealthy and powerful patrons outside the community. This in turn led to personal doubt, dissimulation, despair, and defection. The community was suffering an erosion of integrity and cohesion at the personal and social levels of life. The problem in today's verses is social and communal. Community members are discriminating against others and showing partiality to the rich. The solution is to refrain from showing partiality.

The word translated "assembly" is literally "synagogue." This not only indicates the mixed nature of this community but is a unique example in the New Testament of the retention of a Judean term and concept for describing a gathering of folk who have accepted Jesus as Messiah (compare Matt 4:23, "their synagogues," implying a difference from "our synagogues"). Moreover, in this hypothetical example, the two visitors are strangers to the assembly, and their status can be surmised only from their garments. The instruction is that God has chosen the poor rooted in the conviction that the poor are objects of God's special care (Ps 35:10), a notion familiar from the gospel (Matt 5:3; Luke 6:20). As such the poor are heirs of the kingdom.

Today's gospel (Mark 7:31-37) recounts Jesus' healing of a deaf mute. The divided community which received the letter of James also needed to have their ears opened. If the ears of modern believers are closed to divisive behaviors in the community, who will open them, and how?

Twenty-Fourth Sunday in Ordinary Time
James 2:14-18

In this third contrast, the sacred author highlights negative communal behavior (lack of faith-in-action toward the needy, 2:14-17) with the positive ideal (show faith through action, 2:18-26). Faith in this context means the free acceptance of God's saving activity on behalf of human beings, and works refers to the obedient implementation of God's saving will in every aspect of life. The specific focus here is on "speaking-completed-in-doing," that is, the mouth/ears symbolic body zone (see also Jas 1:13, 19, 26; 2:3, 7, 12, 14-26; 3:1-12, 14; 4:3, 11-12, 13-17; 5:9, 12, 13-18). Since all zones are expected to work harmoniously in a healthy and whole person, it is not enough to say nice things without also doing whatever is necessary to bring the nice things to fruition. If good works do not implement faith, it is dead. Such faith is the exact opposite of the kind described by Paul as "faith working through love" (Gal 5:6).

Situated in the cultural world of the Eastern Mediterranean, this discussion is hardly unusual. In this world, the ideal is more important than the real. Since honor depends on an external show of work, external perception, and public approval, what one says is valued more highly than what one does. This is because deeds often don't measure up to what one claims. Contemporary Bedouins agree that the son who responded politely to his father and said what the father wanted to hear, though he had no intention of going to work in his father's vineyard, behaved more honorably than the other son who publicly insulted his father (Matt 21:28-30). The natives of Jesus' time also knew the correct answer to his question in v. 30: Who did the will of the father? For them, however, the ideal is more important than the real; what one says is more important than what one does. This is why throughout Matthew's gospel Jesus insists that doing the right thing is equally important as knowing and saying it (7:21-23; 12:46-50).

Another cultural dimension of today's verses is the argument in v. 18. This is an agonistic society, prone to conflict. The sacred author does not hesitate to cast his instruction into the form of an argument. Some community members specialize in faith, others in works. The author sides with those who are perceived to focus on works alone. "I will demonstrate my faith to you," which underlies my works.

It is difficult to relate this reading to the gospel (Mark 8:27-35) where the topic is not so much about saying the right thing as it is about the high cultural value placed on secrecy. While Peter does indeed say the right thing about him, Jesus' advice not to tell anyone is normal and not part of a literary strategy in Mark (the so-called Messianic secret). Mediterranean males in particular specialize in "making oneself out to be" characterized by this or that quality, etc. Since there is confusion in the populace, and all guesses (including Peter's) about Jesus' identity actually honor him, Jesus makes the appropriate cultural decision. Shh! Keep it quiet. Life becomes more difficult as people learn more about a person.

Given that the verses of today's epistolary reading contain an inclusion (vv. 14, 18 = faith, without works), it could be possible to interpret Jesus' concern in the gospel as a caution that if the populace did indeed know his identity as Messiah, their interpretation (according to what Jesus adds) would be incorrect, and therefore the actions based on misunderstanding would be wrong-headed.

Twenty-Fifth Sunday in Ordinary Time
James 3:16–4:3

Today the architects of the lectionary combine elements from the fourth exhortation in this letter (3:1-18) with the negative statement from the fifth exhortation (4:1-4). Avoid jealousy and selfish ambition (negative), but act rather with the pure, peaceful wisdom from above (positive; vv. 16-18). Do not pursue selfish desire which leads to enmity with fellow human beings and with God (negative; 4:1-4). These combined verses also join two of three interrelated dimensions of human life that the sacred author has in mind throughout this letter: the social (4:1-4) and the cosmic (3:14-18; the third dimension is the personal). Each of these dimensions of life is permeated with the same problem: a contrast and conflict between attitudes, values, actions, and agents representing wholeness, unity, and purity on the one hand, with attitudes, values, actions, and agents representing incompleteness, disunity, and pollution on the other.

Personal attitudes such as jealousy and selfish ambition spawn disorder and every foul practice. The Greek word translated here as jealousy is rendered as zeal in John 2:17: "Zeal for your house will consume me." A citation from Ps 69:9 describes a positive quality: defensive protection of God's honor and reputation. Indeed, in Greek literature such "good" jealousy characterizes "the haves" who are concerned to defend their possessions: family, property, or reputation. But here in Jas 3:14, 16 (also in Acts 5:17; 7:9; 13:45; Rom 13:13; 1 Cor 3:3; 13:4; 2 Cor 12:20; Gal 5:20) that same Greek word has a negative meaning: evil, hostile action toward others, an attack on others. These attitudes (jealousy, selfish ambition) represent earthly, unspiritual, demonic "wisdom." The preferable attitudes derive from wisdom from above which is pure, peaceable, gentle, reasonable, full of mercy and good fruits, without uncertainty or insincerity. The two contending wisdoms, devilish and divine (from above), derive from the cosmic dimension. Believers should embrace the divine and eschew devilish wisdom.

The social consequence of these opposed sources and forms of wisdom is two contrasting societies: an antagonistic and divided society animated by devilish wisdom from below (described in 4:1-4), and a peaceful and integral society animated by divine wisdom from above (described in 4:7-10). Ultimately it is the devil (4:4-10) and an earthly, unspiritual, devilish wisdom from below (3:14-16) that pervade society (1:27). This inspires double-mindedness, duplicity, doubt, social discrimination, division, discord, disloyalty to God, pollution, and death. In contrast, God and wisdom from above are the sources of purity, peace, integrity, and life (3:17-18; 4:4-10). Simultaneous allegiance to these alternative realms fragments and polarizes the community.

Today's gospel (Mark 9:30-37) reports the disciples debating among themselves "who is the greatest." On the face of it, this sounds like something very appropriate in a society where honor is the core value, but in the zero-sum game that life is in an honor-driven culture, this kind of concern is divisive and destructive. The author of James spells out in greater detail why this is so. Western culture, which encourages individuals to have "vanity walls" (a place to display all one's achievements), may find such a concern trivial. What analogous threat to community exists in Western contexts, and how would one defend against it?

Twenty-Sixth Sunday in Ordinary Time
James 5:1-6

This final reading from James reports a negative behavior, namely, oppression of laborers and the just by the rich (5:1-6). The balancing, positive advice is: wait patiently for the Lord's coming and be steadfast (5:7-11). These are clearly behaviors in the social dimension that can work for ill or good.

Modern Western readers whose focal social institution is economics, especially as formulated and developed by Karl Marx and Adam Smith, must realize that it is anachronistic and disrespectful to impose these ideas on today's verse. "Rich" in the Bible is not primarily an indicator of economic standing. It can have many meanings depending on context, but basically it designates people who belong to the urban elite, who hold high status accompanied by power, influence, and great wealth. Notice that status brings power and wealth, quite the opposite from the West in which wealth brings status and power. In the biblical world, status (deriving primarily from birth) was more important than money. Toll collectors might have had money, but they did not have status.

As today's reading indicates (fields, harvesting, fattening, and slaughter, vv. 4, 5), owning land and cattle gave a person high status in antiquity and, of course, brought in wealth. The reference to wealth that has rotted (v. 2) could be a reference to poor crops, poor harvest, or stored grain that has indeed rotted. Status requires "conspicuous consumption" so that everyone will know that person is wealthy. Status also requires associating with others of like status. To accomplish this, one needs resources routinely gained by withholding just wages from those who make the elite life possible (see Lev 19:13; Deut 24:14). In addition, status is signaled by attire, another "expense" of keeping others aware of one's status (see Matt 6:9; Acts 20:33).

But the wealth that status helps to accumulate easily builds up to surplus, and surplus entails a new obligation: to become a patron, that is, to distribute surplus wealth to people in need who become clients. These clients in turn would proclaim the benevolence of the benefactor, thereby increasing his reputation and adding to real "wealth," namely, honor and status. If the "rich" do not pay wages due, then clearly they also refuse to be patrons (the problem in Luke 12:15-21). Shameful in their culture, such persons are damnable in God's eyes. The final verse (6) may be an allusion to Sir 34:22: "He slays his neighbor who deprives him of his living; he sheds blood who denies the laborer his wages."

Scholars do not think these verses reflect an actual situation in the community but rather are a generic warning of the challenges accompanying high status, known to one and all but often neglected. There is a very tenuous connection (perhaps intended by the architects of the lectionary) between this reading from James and today's gospel (Mark 9:38-43, 45, 47-48): the word "fire." A stronger relationship is Jesus' remark: "Anyone who gives you a cup of water to drink because you belong to Christ . . . will surely not lose his reward." The reading from James sharpens the focus. In our society where donations to charity are tax-deductible, and aid to the poor and needy can be shared in the most anonymous and antiseptic fashion, what insights do today's readings offer?

Twenty-Seventh Sunday in Ordinary Time
Hebrews 2:9-11

[For introductory comments see Nativity: Mass during the Day.] A central theme of most of Hebrews is the priestly act by which Jesus effected "purification from sins" (1:3, revised NAB). Once again the architects of the lectionary have exercised creative surgery in preparing this reading for today's liturgy. First, they have mixed two segments of this Scripture. Verse 9 concludes the sacred author's interpretation of Ps 8:4-6 which began in Heb 2:6. Verse 10 begins a segment (2:10-18) that reflects upon high priestly perfection through suffering. Torn from context and recombined to form today's reading, these verses remain intelligible, but one can only lament for the sacred author who wrote an integral composition with diligence and care.

In v. 9, the sacred author has creatively reinterpreted Psalm 8 which said that human beings are "a little bit" beneath the divine and has applied it to Jesus saying that "for a little while" Jesus shared fully (not just a little bit) in the human condition, including human suffering and death. But this temporary subjection was following by a "crowning with glory and honor" (a phrase from v. 9 curiously omitted from today's reading!). The savior's mission culminates in his death and exaltation, which leads naturally into the next verses explaining how the savior led many children to glory.

109

It was God's will that Jesus, as leader of many children to glory, should accomplish this through suffering, which makes possible life in the new covenant. The Greek word translated as "leader" has many meanings in Greek literature, but here is best interpreted as a "guide" along a path to heaven (a notion common in Greek, Israelite, and Gnostic sources). Through his suffering, Jesus the guide becomes the perfect model of obedience, and the perfect intercessor who is merciful and faithful.

Finally, since Jesus and his followers (the one who consecrates and those who are consecrated) have one origin, God, whose saving plan is directed to all human beings with whom Jesus is in solidarity by reason of his humanity, Jesus is not ashamed to call fellow humans brothers and sisters. This kinship terminology was very common outside the Gospels (e.g., Rom 1:13; 8:12, 29; Acts 1:15; 20:23; 11:1) perhaps because Jesus called his disciples brothers (see Matt 28:10; John 20:17).

Today's gospel (Mark 10:2-16) illustrates the depth of Jesus' humanity. He became incarnate in the ancient Mediterranean world, specifically in Israelite society. We hear him reflecting upon and refining the possibility of divorce in that tradition. We also see him upholding the role of children in that culture as "snoops" and gossip purveyors who must have the freedom to explore all "suspicious" adult behaviors so that they might report back to their families whether these are potentially threatening to family security and integrity. The sacred author of Hebrews reminds us that God honored Jesus for his good life, and God through Jesus will lead Jesus' "brothers and sisters" to the same honor. What more could one possibly want in life?

Twenty-Eighth Sunday in Ordinary Time
Hebrews 4:12-13

This elaborate piece of florid prose brings to a conclusion the theme of God's speech which has been a major theme in the opening chapters of this letter. Human beings in all cultures fully understand the power of speech, particularly the fact that its effects are difficult if not impossible to undo. Appreciation for the effectiveness of a human word in Middle Eastern culture is rooted in the way in which young boys are raised. The customary marriage partner for the young man, a father's brother's daughter, traditionally leaves her home of origin to move in with her spouse, who will continue to live after marriage in the complex of his father. (Peter's house in Capernaum and Jesus' "home" there were in the complex of Jonah, the father of Simon and Andrew.) Even though the bride is a relative, she is not fully integrated into the family until she bears a son (see 1 Sam 1:8). This not only gives a secure place in the family but is also social security for life. The birth of a son is a great joy for all. The youngster is brought up in the women's quarters by all the women (mother, sisters, and the rest) and is pampered. Boys are traditionally breast-fed twice as long as girls and weaned around age three (see 2 Macc 7:27) long after the boy can speak. The young boy soon learns the power of his word. All he needs to say is "Feed me," and he gets fed. It is no stretch of the imagination for such a boy to grow up and write Genesis 1 where God creates by simply commanding it.

This is the cultural background that helps to interpret this reflection on God's word which indeed is living, effective, sharper than a two-edged sword, creative (Gen 1:3; Isa 55:11), and judgmental (Amos 1:2; Ps 51:6). This latter is the sacred author's point here. God's judgment is heightened by another cultural insight. Human beings in this culture are not only non-introspective but anti-introspective. No one believes a human being knows what is going on in the heart of another or even one's own heart. Only God knows that (1 Sam 16:7). Thus only God can read hearts, and no secrecy, lying, or deception can distract God as it can fellow human beings. As Jesus reminds his disciples in today's gospel (Mark 10:17-30), nothing is impossible for God. Both readings offer a heartening message to believers of every age. God renders just judgments, and God is truly in charge of life.

Twenty-Ninth Sunday in Ordinary Time
Hebrews 4:14-16

These verses conclude the section that began in 3:1 in which Jesus and Moses, the faithful son and faithful servant, have been compared. In particular, there are two exhortations in these verses: let us hold fast to our confession; let us confidently approach the throne of grace.

The confession refers to a formal statement of belief: Jesus is the Son of God. He has been exalted as a great high priest having passed through the path (the sky or the many heavens) that leads to God's throne (v. 16), the place of Jesus' exaltation. The association of incarnation and humiliation (he knew our weaknesses which lead us—but not him!—to sin; v. 15) with his exaltation repeats a motif that has been sounded in the first two chapters.

The throne of grace, or the throne of God who bestows grace, is a constellation in the sky (Isa 66:1: "Thus says the Lord: the sky is my throne"). The whole sky is God's throne (Matt 5:34; 23:22; 1 Enoch 14:51-24). This is where Jesus has been exalted, and it is the place where believers can expect to receive mercy and find grace for timely help. Mercy is a value in Mediterranean culture by which persons are expected to meet their interpersonal obligations. When sick people ask Jesus for mercy, they ask that he do for them what he can: obtain remission of sin, restore to well-being.

The same is now true of the exalted Jesus. Grace is a result of a covenant or contract between unequals: parents and children, husband and wife or wives, patron and client, helper and accident victim. By reason of being patron to human beings who are clients, God "owes" life or sustains the life of clients who are said to "receive mercy." Thus from a cultural perspective, the terms are nearly synonymous, but the meaning is clear. Because of who Jesus our high priest is (Son of God) and what he has accomplished (solidarity with us, but did not sin), we can confidently obtain what we need.

In effect, this is what Jesus says in today's gospel (Mark 10:35-45). To James and John who ask for a share in his ultimate glory, Jesus replies that it is not his to give, but his Father's to grant to those for whom it has been prepared. The author of Hebrews illuminates what has been made available. How can this message not inspire confidence?

Thirtieth Sunday in Ordinary Time
Hebrews 5:1-6

The citation of Ps 2:7 in Heb 5:5 and Heb 1:5 forms an inclusio or inclusion for this part of the letter. This is a literary device (repetition of words or ideas) signaling the author's intention explicitly manifest in the text that this text-segment should be considered as a unit. Similarly "the one who said" (v. 5) echoes the phrase "God spoke" in 1:1, further strengthening the inclusion. The theme in this segment has been Jesus' status as divine Son.

Today's text-segment focuses on Jesus as High Priest and makes three general points of comparison between the high priest described in the Bible (see Exodus 28–29; Leviticus 8–10; Deut 33:8-11; Sir 45:6-22; 50:1-22) and Jesus as High Priest. To appreciate the comparisons, some cultural information about intermediaries might help. Ordinarily in this culture people dealt with one another by means of dyadic relationships that included informal agreements to reciprocating each other's favors. But when equals (who alone are capable of this kind of relationship) are unable to meet another's needs, then a needy person seeks a patron, a person of means or who has surplus which allows him to meet the needs of clients. The intermediary in this relationship is a broker, someone who has no clients, but puts clients in touch with patrons.

A related function of an intermediary is to be a mediator, that is, someone who can intervene between feuding parties, or parties at odds with each other, in order to restore a harmonious relationship. Ideally in this culture, a mediator should not be related to either party, or if related should be at least five links removed. The reason for this is to render the mediator's judgment acceptable to both feuding or alienated parties. This is the idea behind the makarism: "How truly honorable are the peacemakers [= mediators], for they shall be called sons of God" (Matt 5:9). Mediators quell feuds which can too easily escalate to violence, proceed to bloodshed, and result in blood-feud which is very difficult to halt.

The first point of comparison is that a high priest is an ordinary human being appointed by God to be an intermediary (or mediator) who would make "gifts and sacrifices for sins" to the deity. In other words, when God is shamed (which is what sin does to God) and is justified in seeking redress, God's appointed mediator steps in to restrain the justified and deserved punishment. The second point of comparison is the ability of such a human mediator to empathize with human failings of this nature relative to God. Due to human nature, the mediator sometimes must act on his own behalf as he does on behalf of others. The high priest/mediator thus should show patient restraint with sinners. The third and final point of comparison is that God selects and calls the intermediary; no human being dare assume it (see Exod 28:1; though in the Maccabean period, candidates did compete and bid for the honor from the Seleucids).

Verses 5-6 demonstrate that Jesus the High Priest is superior on all counts. God designated the Son as High Priest. Just as Ps 2:7 attributed priestly status to a king, so the sacred author attributes an eternal priesthood to the Son (Ps 110 [109]:4; compare Heb 5:10; 6:20; 7:17, 21) who, of course, is fully human and totally pleasing to the Father.

In his healing ministry (Mark 10:46-52, today's gospel), Jesus was a broker for sick clients with God their healing patron. The glorified Jesus as High Priest now does even more for God's people. Westerners accustomed to self-service or even representing themselves in judicial proceedings might feel inclined to "do it themselves" with God. Who would want to run that risk?

Thirty-First Sunday in Ordinary Time
Hebrews 7:23-28

An inclusio or inclusion (the word "oath" is repeated) in vv. 20 and 28 identifies this final unit of five reflections on Melchizedek (7:1-3, 4-10, 11-19, 20-25, 26-28). Melchizedek is mentioned only twice in the Bible (see Genesis 14 and Psalm 110), a fact which helps a reader to appreciate the creative interpretations of the sacred author of Hebrews. The sacred author uses this motif of oath to draw contrasts between Jesus and the Levitical priests in three segments. First (vv. 20-22), the author works God's oath in Psalm 110 to show that this creates not a superior priesthood but rather a better covenant.

Today's verses contain the fourth and fifth reflections. Verses 23-24 sound the theme of abiding life. The fact that Jesus' priesthood is eternal (unlike Levitical priests who had to be replaced upon death) means there are no gaps. Jesus is always there to intercede with God for his followers.

The final segment (vv. 26-28) concludes the reflections on Jesus' priesthood which is patterned after the "order of Melchizedek." It makes two main points: Jesus' priesthood abides, Levites come and go; and Jesus' priestly status is confirmed by God's oath. The first three of the five adjectives describing Jesus the High Priest can describe Levitical high priests as well. The last two are distinctive. Jesus is separated from sinners—especially those who could oppose him—by his exalted location higher than the sky. Further, while Levitical priests offered many sacrifices, Jesus' was once for all.

The importance of God's oath might fail to make an impression on modern Western readers. In Middle Eastern cultures, lying and deception are legitimate strategies for preserving one's honor and reputation. Since all God-talk is based on human experience which is culturally fashioned, the praiseworthy trait of deception in the service of honor is something at which God would be considered to excel. Human beings in this culture certify they are telling the truth by making an oath, hence this fantastic news about an extraordinary High Priest could be seen as a ploy by God to preserve his honorable reputation (see 1 Kgs 22:23 in context). God therefore uses an oath to assure the reality and reliability of a perfect son who functions as High Priest on behalf of sinners.

In today's gospel (Mark 12:28b-34), Jesus scores love of God and neighbor as "worth more than all burnt offerings and sacrifices." Today's reading from Hebrews illustrates the value of what Jesus accomplished by his sacrifice motivated by love of the Father and fellow human beings. How blessed are believers to have such a loving brother and impressive model to emulate.

Thirty-Second Sunday in Ordinary Time
Hebrews 9:24-28

Once again the sacred author returns to the imagery of Yom Kippur, the Day of Atonement (see Leviticus 16), as a type of the death of Jesus. On this day, the high priest sacrificed a bull for his own sins and those of the people. Then he entered the Holy of Holies to incense the "mercy seat," the place from which God dispensed mercy to his people, and to sprinkle it with blood from the bull. Next he slaughtered a goat for the sins of the people and sprinkled some of that on the mercy seat, too. The sacred author contrasts with this the sacrifice of Jesus: he died just once, which allowed him entry to the presence of God (which is what the mercy seat symbolized) in the sky. The blood of this sacrifice is not that of animals but of Jesus' sacrifice of his life. The effect is Jesus took away sin, once and for all. At his second appearance he will bring salvation which has already been initiated to its final consummation. The judgment that follows death mentioned in v. 27 is probably a good link with today's gospel (Mark 12:38-44) in which Jesus critiques the scribes for teaching the widow (and others) to impoverish herself, something even the culture did not approve of or tolerate. How fortunate to have the patronage of an effective High Priest whose sacrifice took away sin. How tragic to realize that sometimes even God's representatives neglect this gift and mislead the people in their care.

Thirty-Third Sunday in Ordinary Time
Hebrews 10:11-14, 18

These verses bring to a conclusion the presentation of Jesus' priestly act which began in Heb 8:1. It offers no new insight but rather repeats what has already become familiar in these readings. While all priests (the High Priest and all others) repeatedly offered sacrifices, they never removed sin. Jesus the High Priest offered one effective sacrifice and then took his rightful place at God's right hand, a place of honor and authority. The present tense (those who are being consecrated) designates an on-going activity. Believers of all time continue to appropriate the eternal effects of Jesus' sacrifice. Jesus' work is ended; his followers have much to do. Yet, as the concluding verse indicates, those who have received forgiveness need no longer make offerings for sin. The gospel (Mark 13:24-32) offers the heartening news that when the Son of Man returns he will send out his messengers who will gather his elect, those who embraced the effects of his ever-effective sacrifice to be with him forever.

Thirty-Fourth Sunday in Ordinary Time (Christ the King)
Revelation 1:5-8

The book of Revelation is the record of John's experiences in altered states of consciousness. He is an astral seer who professes faith in the resurrected Jesus, but he also maintains that he belongs to the house of Israel. The visions took place over an extended period of time. Some preceded the destruction of Jerusalem in A.D. 70, while others were experienced after this date. Obviously, the final edition of this book was sometime after A.D. 70. The basic format of the book is a letter (1:4–3:22; 20:11–22:21) into which various visions have been inserted (4:1–11:19; 12:1–16:21; 17:1–20:10; 21:1–22:5). In vision, John experienced the cosmic Son of Man who gave edicts to the angels of seven Asian Jesus-groups while he was on the island of Patmos, off the coast of Ephesus (Western Turkey).

Today's verses are drawn from the opening of the letter (1:4-5, 7-8) and feature traditional elements. There is a greeting (4c-5a) and a thanksgiving directed to God (vv. 5b-6). The greeting comes from Jesus Messiah introduced in kinship terms—firstborn of the dead—and in political terms—the first ruler of the earth. The blessing or thanksgiving that follows (vv. 5b-6) acknowledges what was done in the past (loved us, freed us from sins by his blood, made us into a kingdom, priests for his God and Father). It also sends wishes for good things in the immediate future (vv. 7-8). He is coming soon just as he went (Acts 1:9): by means of clouds. When he comes, all will mourn. Mourning refers to a ritual action intended to protest the presence of evil (e.g., see 1 Cor 5:2). Usually this is done by prayer, fasting, wearing sackcloth and ashes, depriving oneself of sleep (usually called vigil). The fact that all will mourn indicates that Jesus' death was an evil act.

The final verse presents a divine pronouncement from the Lord God. He identifies himself as the first and last letter of the Greek alphabet. Since only 2 percent of the population at the time were literate, John's message is not for ordinary people. Few knew the alphabet, and fewer still knew how to manipulate the letters of the alphabet for purposes of divination. Thus the hidden meaning of these letters reveals something about God. God's name tells us who God really is, hence this is a full disclosure of God's essence. This is why it must remain hidden and mysterious, for if a person knew that name he would have power over God.

The gospel for this feast (John 18:33b-37) recounts the scene in which Jesus is identified as King of Judeans. He concludes: "for this I was born and for this I came into the world, to testify to the truth." In Revelation, the risen and cosmic Jesus is going to testify to the truth for John the astral prophet. How blessed to have a friend like Jesus to lead us to truth.

Recommended Resources

Elliot, John H. "The Epistle of James in Rhetorical and Social Scientific Perspective: Holiness–Wholeness." *Biblical Theology Bulletin* 23 (1993) 71–81.

Malina, Bruce J., and John J. Pilch. *Social Science Commentary on the Book of Revelation*. Minneapolis: Fortress Press, 2000.

Malina, Bruce J., and Jerome H. Neyrey. *Portraits of Paul: An Archaeology of Ancient Personality*. Louisville, Ky.: Westminster John Knox Press, 1996.

Murphy-O'Connor, Jerome. *Paul: A Critical Life*. New York and Oxford: Oxford University Press, 1997.

_____. *Paul the Letter-Writer: His World, His Options, His Skills*. Collegeville: The Liturgical Press, 1995.

Neyrey, Jerome H. *Paul in Other Words: A Cultural Reading of His Letters*. Louisville, Ky.: Westminster John Knox Press, 1994.

Pilch, John J. *The Cultural Dictionary of the Bible*. Collegeville: The Liturgical Press, 1999.

_____. *The Cultural World of Jesus Sunday by Sunday: Cycle B*. Collegeville: The Liturgical Press, 1996.

_____. *Galatians and Romans*. The Collegeville Bible Commentary 6. Collegeville: The Liturgical Press, 1982.

_____. "Illuminating the World of Jesus through Cultural Anthropology." *The Living Light* 31 (1994) 20–31. http://www.georgetown. edu/faculty/pilchj/ click on: "Mediterranean Culture."

_____. *The Triduum: Breaking Open the Scriptures.* Collegeville: The Liturgical Press, 2000.

Sloyan, Gerard S. "What Kind of Canon Do the Lectionaries Constitute?" *Biblical Theology Bulletin* 30 (2000) 27–35.

Websites

Roman Catholic Lectionary for Mass:
http://clawww.lmu.edu/faculty/fjust/Lectionary.htm

Revised Common Lectionary:
http://divinity.library.vanderbilt.edu/lectionary